Bernd Degen

The Discus – King of the Aquarium

Bernd Degen

,,The Discus – King of the Aquarium"

A reference book for
the Discus lover

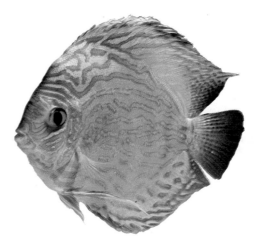

© Original 1986 by Bede-Verlag, Kollnburg, West Germany
All rights reserved
Print: Vereinigte Oberpfälzische Druckereien und Verlagsanstalt GmbH, Amberg, West Germany.
Library of congress catalog No. 87-050983
ISBN 3-923880-95-2

Photographs:
G. Blecha, Witten-Stockum Discus Centre
Pages 10/16/71 bottom
Stefanski Discus Centre, Waltrop
Pages 11/18/21/44–45/52–53/67/69 bottom
Arbogast/Bergs, Page 16 left
K. Erfurt, Pages 73/99 bottom
Michael Degen, Page 55

K. H. Schmidt, Page 16 right
H. Hoffmann, Page 17
Dennerle, Vinningen, Page 33
U. Heinrichs, Page 39
J. Nemec, Page 63
K. H. Ring, Page 79 top

All other photos and title pictures by Bernd Degen
Translated by Eberhard Schulze, London

English language distributors:
TETRA PRESS, 201 Tabor Rd., Morris Plains, N.J. 07950
Rolf C. Hagen, Inc., 3225 Sartelon St., Montreal, Quebec H4R 1E8, Canada
Warner-Lambert Pet Care (Tetra), Mitchell House, Southampton Road, Eastleigh, Hampshire S05 5RY, England
WL-Code: 16034

Contents

Foreword

When I finished writing ,,Das neue Diskus-buch" in 1984 I hardly imagined that there were so many Discus-lovers. The book was quickly sold out and the idea was born of writing a new, finer Discus book. It was supported by countless Discus friends who with enthusiastic letters and telephone calls asked for this, second book. That is how this fine Discus book I am now offering you came about. It will help you to re-appreciate the beauty of this true ,,King of the Aquarium". It will also, however, give chapter and verse on keeping and breeding these fishes. And not least, it is sufficiently comprehensive to ensure that more and more aquarists will turn to the Discus. Once infected by Discus fever, there is no escape.

This book was conceived with love. I hope it will give you much pleasure and also help to secure the future of our Discus fish in the aquarium. But I hope, too, that the book will help you to get to know the Discus even better as a lovable, domestic pet.

A Thank You

is what I should like to offer all my Discus friends and aquaintances who have helped me in all the various ways in writing this book. Whether because they wrote me a letter or spoke to me on the telephone. Because they discussed the fish with me or allowed me to photograph their Discus aquarium.

My special thanks go to my Discus friend Dieter Putz of Pilsting, with whom I spent many a hour in front of the Discus tank. Thanks, also, to Uwe Heinrichs of Essen for his fine slides and text ,,A beginner's first experiences".

And a big thanks to all the photographers who sent me their finest Discus photos so that this book can show off some of the finest specimens.

And a quite special thanks to the many readers of my first Discus book ,,Das neue Diskus-buch". Had you not ,,devoured" this book in so few months, this second book would certainly never have followed so fast on its heels.

Bernd Degen

Bernd Degen

A Beginner's First Experiences

In the beginning, there was quite unnatural respect for this true King of the Aquarium, the Discus. These splendid cichlids were always my dream fish as an aquarist. Now the dream was at last to become reality! Three Heckel Discus were the start. However, theirs was a dull existence in a well planted-up community tank with Neons, Angels, Catfishes and a few other species. My joy with the Discus fish was short-lived, and no doubt as with me, so it was with many other beginners. But now, ambition and curiosity for this new fish had me in thrall. To begin with, I read everything about Discus I could lay my hands on. The community tank was converted to a pure Discus tank with plants. The Angels and Neons had to go. I took time to set up the aquarium and to prepare the water, which was soon to accommodate my new treasures, five half-grown Royal-Blues. Through careful, frequent feeding and regular part-water changes, problems in keeping were carefully avoided.

Now the Discus took hold. The tanks became ever more numerous and larger. The Discus fish ever more splendorous and, unfortunately, more expensive. No distance was too great to obtain these fine fish.

Before long, my hobby was crowned by a 125 gallons (500 litre) tank in the living room, with 8 adult Turquoise Discus. Everything had been achieved? But really everything? No, because the next step was to breed from these fish. But until that happened a great deal of time was to pass and much money was to be spent on acquiring experience. When searching for suitable breeding pairs I soon found that this was a road set with snares and pitfalls. But even here, obstinacy was rewarded. My prize was a real pair of Turquoise. After a fortnight, the fishes courted and spawned. Almost hour by hour I went to the tank to see how many eggs were gathering mould, because this is really a fearful time for the Discus breeder. I was lucky and many fry hatched from the first clutch. But it was to be of short duration because the same evening they became free-swimming all the young suddenly disappeared. The solution to the riddle was the filter. It had simply sucked up the fry.

The next clutch was not long in coming and this time everything ran to perfection. After 5 weeks I had fished more than 100 young Discus from the tank and transferred them to a breeding aquarium. Many broods were to follow. Today, the Discus is no longer a mystery to me, but it is still the most fascinating of aquarium-dwellers and one which gives the attentive keeper much joy.

The Discus Fish from 1840 to the present

A fine Turquoise Discus bred from an established line. This specimen passes all its good qualities to its progeny.

1840 is the magic date for the discovery of the Discus. The Viennese ichthyologist Dr. Johann Jacob Heckel described a specimen in Natterer's collection as Symphysodon discus. In Dr. Heckel's honour, this fish is now still called the Heckel Discus in aquarists' language. It was not until 1930 that the first Discus were imported into Germany and the USA. Even then, only few, select aquarists had the opportunity of acquiring them. Whether they succeeded in breeding them we do not know. All that subsequent reports say is that the Discus behaves much like the Angel-fish in its reproductive capacity. That, too, was probably the reason why it still took so long before progeny was successfully obtained from the Discus.

In the early days of Discus keeping, eggs were actually taken away from the parent fish to protect them from the latter. Attempts were made to raise Discus artificially, as had of course already been done with Angels.

Only in the sixties did the first information about Discus fish reach the aquarist journals. At the same time, the airline connections with the fish collecting stations in the South American jungle were improved. It then became possible to despatch fish worldwide from Iquitos in Peru, Leticia in Colombia and Manaus and Belem in Brazil. The range of Discus was soon broadened and this paved the way for the wildcatch boom of the seventies. It was then the basis was laid for the quality fish available in the German market today. These are the kind of fish which tireless breeders have spent long years raising to a standard of quality which must be amongst the best worldwide. From fish generation to fish generation, the colours have been more strongly highlighted, while netheless largely retaining the typical Discus shape, so that today we have Turquoise Discus, in particular, swimming in the aquariums of hobbyists which are at the summit of their class.

The Amazonian Habitat

The habitat of our Discus fish embraces parts of Brazil, Peru, Colombia and Venezuela. A gigantic rain forest area with numerous large rivers almost beyond the powers of imagination. Many of these Amazon rivers rise in the Andes.

The rivers are divided into three types, depending on the kind of water – the white water, black water and clear water areas. The best known and largest are the white water rivers of the Amazon, including the Solimoes, the Rio Madeira, and the Rio Branco. Important clear water rivers are the Rio Tapajos and Rio Xingu. Black waters are found in the Rio Negro and Rio Cururu.

White water rivers with turbid, loam-yellow water offer visibility of only a few inches (centimetres). These white water rivers carry rich sediments to the Amazon. The silt is transported from the Andes right down to the Atlantic. This white water has a pH value of just below 7. Its conductivity, at 30 to 60 μS, is still the highest of any type of water.

Because of the large quantities of deposited matter which these rivers carry with them the banks undergo continuous change.

Black water rivers are coloured an olive to dark brown and are rather more transparent. Visibility is possible to depths of 5 ft. (1.50 m). Their conductivity, at 10 to 20 μS, is very low and the pH value, too, is at between 4 and 5 at the bottom end of the scale.

Clear water rivers, with their greenish colour, have the highest transparency. Here, visibility has been measured to depths of 4 yd. (4 m) approx. Like the black water rivers, they also have an unfavourably low electrolyte content, expressed in a conducticity of less than 15 μS. The pH value is usually between 5 and 6.

Huge areas of the Amazon are flooded each year during the rainy season. These floods offer

Catching station on the Amazon. From here the Aborigines set out to catch Discus.

Turquoise and Royal Blue Discus hide amongst the dense tangle of plants. This means much work for the catcher in netting them.

Here a Discus pair have found each other.
The colours do not match too well, as the
male is a plain blue and the female a Red/
Turquoise. Yet these fishes fitted in so
harmoniously and got on so well together
that it seemed a shame to separate them.

Plain Cobalt Blue Discus, like this beefy male are high in the popularity stakes. Breeders aim at an absolutely even body colour. Line markings may appear only in the head region.

the fish good spawning conditions in newly created small waters. High water temperatures produced by the strong sunlight on these small ponds encourage the Discus to spawn. At the same time many Infusoria appear, who together with all types of micro life offer the young fish an abundance of food. In these waters, to which the trees' shade does not extend, temperatures may rise to 90° F (32° C) so that the Discus enjoy ideal conditions for spawning. This knowledge can also be usefully applied to our discus aquariums.

The heavy rainfall in the Amazon area starts in December. The rivers then reach their highwater levels in January and February. Floods occur which continue until June. The lowest water levels occur in October and November. The Discus are caught in the narrower backwaters of the Amazon during the rainy season. The main period for exporting wild-caught Discus is October to March. No exports take place in May to August. Catching Discus is heavy work. The traditional method with the fixed net demands a good deal of preparation and work afterwards. The nets are staked out while the area enclosed is freed of driftwood, roots and branches. Once this heavy, laborious work has been done, the nets can be pulled in to obtain the rewards of the labour. Catching Discus at night is also popular. The fish are then sought with a pocket torch, dazzled and gathered in. The enormous increase in the cost of fuel, both for aircraft and for boats, has had a detrimental effect on Discus catching.

The European market is also at a disadvantage as many Discus from the Amazon basin are sent to the USA. The European market for wild-caught Discus has clearly deteriorated in recent years.

Freshly caught fish are kept in these fixed nets during the catching expedition.

Species Description, Classification, Popular Names

Brown Discus – Symphysodon aequifasciatus axelrodi

Heckel Discus – Symphysodon discus Heckel

Although with only four species of Discus there is little to classify, the differences are not easily described. Many pages of scientific discussion has been devoted to this in the text books, the end result of which has again been to confuse.

The Discus lover distinguishes between four species of wildcaught Discus. First of all, the Heckel Discus, or Pompadour, scientifically know as Symhysodon discus. This fish is immediately recognised by its thicker fifth body stripe. The first and last of the vertical stripes, too, are more strongly marked. Because of these strong markings, the fish has not been propagated in hobbyists' aquariums. Today, few, if any, home-bred Heckel Discus can be found on the market. Progeny with these vertical stripes are simply unsaleable.

Heckel Discus have very fine base colours which may vary from reddish to turquoise blue. Thickset wild-caught specimens whit a strong blue cast are a feast for the eyes. Crosses with Heckel Discus are therefore popular, especially in Asia, to retain the blue or turquoise lines in the progeny. Attempts to breed away the vertical central stripe have not been entirely successful. Heckel Discus are sold as Pompadour Discus, Blue Heckel and Red Heckel.

The name Brown Discus conceals Symphysodon axelrodi. This wild-caught species was that most frequently found in our hobbyists' tanks in the sixties and seventies. It is practically the ancestor of our presentday Discus fishes. Its basic body colour is a light to dark brown. It has a few blue stripes on its head, back and ventral

Brown Discus and Heckel Discus in a species tank with Neons and Amazon Sword Plants.

fins. The anal fins usually include a fine red. The vertical stripes occur above the eye and are more strongly marked on the caudal fin.

Brown Discus fish with a strong reddish cast in the green are often called Red Discus but this morph occurs only infrequently. No homebred specimens of the pronouncedly Red Discus, whose basic colour is red instead of brown, are known. Young fish, specially from Asia, which are offered as Red Discus have been coloured with special food. The colour disappears when this food is discontinued.

As with all wild-caught Discus, the colour of the eye may proceed from red through orange to yellow. Discus breeders usually go for fish with red eyes.

The third representative of the Discus fish is the Green Discus, Symphysodon aequifasciatus aequifsciatus, also commonly sold as the Pellegrin Discus. The fish was classified by Pellegrin in 1903. The ,,ordinary" Green Discus has a greenybrownish base colour, with green stripes around the back and stomach. Fish striped all over in green or turquoise are known as Pellegrin Discus or, nowadays, also as Royal Green Discus.

A further green variant is the Tefe Discus. The striking features of the Tefe are his first and last vertical bands, which are strongly marked, and numerours red spots which are distributed all over the body, and especially on the stomach. These fish are greatly coveted and at present still very difficult to obtain.

The turquoise-coloured progeny have been raised from sturdy, well-marked wild catches and are now standard. In Germany, in particular, the turquoise-coloured offspring dominate the market.

The fourth type of Discus is the Blue Discus, Symphysodon aequifasciatus haraldi. In its

Faultless Royal Blue wild catches of this quality are seldom imported into Germany today. It owes its name to the continuous blue stripes. Ordinary blue Symphysodon aequifasciatus haraldi caught in the wild are striped only along the upper and lower parts of the body.

base colour it is strongly akin to the Brown Discus. The fish is purple, especially in the head region. Blue longitudinal stripes cover the head, back and stomach. Its overall appearance is most colourful and striking. When fish coloured blue all over were caught, they quickly acquired the name of Royal-Blue. For years they were leaders in the Discus sector. Royal Blues have been and are the epitome of the ,,super''-Discus. Today, fine specimens are rarely found in captivity. The powerful turquoise blue of these wild catches has been retained in their descendants. Homebred specimens are also now available under the name of Cobalt-blue. The ideal in this case is the solid cobalt blue turquoise fish, which is a glossy blue all over. The metallic sheen never fails to fascinate the observer.

The four wild forms of Discus are the ancestors of our homebred varieties. One of our tasks must be to maintain the typical discus shape and the stocky appearance of these fish. With a good round shape and a fine colour, it matters little whether the fish originates from a Blue or a Green Discus. What is important is that the type should not be lost. Large-eyed Discus with gleaming colours but stunted growth cannot be our aim.

Fashionable colours and fantasy markings, repeatedly advocated by certain breeders, are bound to be short-lived. When turquoise-coloured Discus fish display a touch of red in their basic colouring, the error of immediately offering them as Red-turquoise Discus must be avoided. Discus colours depend greatly on the angle of light, water quality, food, the general condition of the fish and other factors. Photos of the same specimens taken shortly after each other soon prove this. The slightest changes in the light will change the picture completely.

Names such as Albino Discus, Electric-blue Discus, Cobalt Discus, Ghost Discus, Peruvian green Discus, Gypsy Discus, Red-pearl Discus and Spotted Blue Discus have come and gone in quick succession.

Discus: From the wild to the aquarium

Even ignoring the large quantities of home-bred Discus, many wild-caught varieties and their offspring still reach home aquariums all oven the world.

The golden age of wild-caught imports is undoubtedly past. In vain, many dealers wait for larger quantities of the fine wild-caught species, since, after all, the magnificent Royal Blue always found a ready market. For the last four or five years, the quality of imported wild catches from Brazil has clearly deteriorated. Ordinary brown and green catches are easier to find, while Tefe or Royal-Blue specimens are virtually unobtainable. Prices, too, have naturally risen, which may ultimately by ascribed to the falling price of the dollar, the increased cost of fuel and the fact that catchers have to travel further and further.

The important exporting stations are in the Brazilian cities of Leticia, Belem and Manaus. Here, the Discus fish which are caught are collected and kept for export. As these fish mean good money to the exporter, particular efforts are taken to keep them in good health. They are prepared for transportation in large plastic containers or tiled tanks. It is important that the intestines should be empty since excrement in the water during transport can produce dramatic changes in its quality. They are therefore no longer fed for several days before despatch. They are then packaged in a double plastic bag, the larger and medium-sized specimens being packaged individually. The transport bag contains just enough water to cover the fish in standing position. By adding oxygen they will tolerate transportation for 48 hours. To avoid fluctuations in temperature the bags are placed in thick polystyrene boxes and carefully sealed. The fish then set off on their long journey in these insulated containers.

When you consider that the fish are packaged several hours before departure and must then be taken to the airport for the customs clearance formalities, that the flight generally takes 10 to 20 hours, that customs takes up a further 2 or 3 hours, and transport to the dealer's tank must also be included, it is not unusual for them to spend 36 to 48 hours in transit. Added to the stress of this long journey it is still the long haul to the hobbyist's tank.

If imported by a wholesaler or large importer, the fish are first accommodated in the importer's installations. From here the road continues, soon after if possible, to the tank of the nearest wholesaler and retailer. Once the fish slowly begin to adjust to their surroundings and to eat properly again, the hobbyist comes along as the last link in this chain and carries the fish to its home aquarium. This, for the time being, is the end of the line.

If the fish has successfully survived so far and we retrace our steps a little, we can see that a wild-caught specimen will usually already have spent four to six weeks in captivity. During this period it has encountered at least three total water changes and a long phase of inadequate food supply. It is now the aquarist's task to nurse the fish back to health and help it recover its full beauty. It goes without saying that the keeper of these wildcaught specimens needs some flair and love for his hobby. Wild catches should therefore be left to the more experienced aquarist. The newcomer is recommended to try his luck with healthy home-bred fish, which need not necessarily be inbred Turquoises.

Many thousands of young Discus are now exported to Europe from Asia, especially from Honk Kong, Bangkok in Thailand and Singapore. Jamaica and Trinidad also export Discus fish. These are almost entirely despatched to the USA.

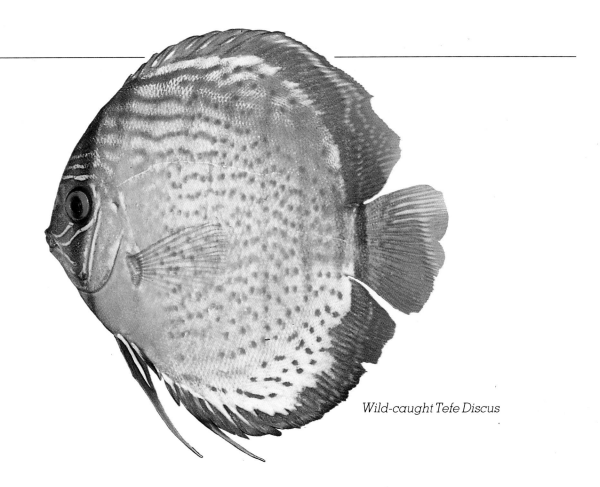

Wild-caught Tefe Discus

The quality of the water in Hongkong, Bangkok and Singapore is ideal for the Discus breeder. It is very soft. In Hong Kong, for example, the pH value is generally over 7 and is reduced for breeding purposes. Gigantic daily water changes from 50% and over offer the fish ideal conditions for breeding and growth. Because of the daily water changes, no filters are used at all. The breeding pairs sit in a small tank often containing only 22 gallons (80 litres). It contains nothing apart from a spawning cone or piece of slate.

Live food is present in abundance, though the type of food differs from one country to another. Tiny water fleas, known as ,,dust Daphnia" are offered to the Discus fry. Apart from tubifex and mosquito larvae, various species of fresh water shrimp feature particulary in the diet. An important food are the eggs of the local crab Macrobrachium rosenbergi, which grows to some 7–8 in. (20 cm). The red-coloured eggs contain a great deal of carotin dye, which when fed to the fry quickly produces a reddish colouring. Of course, they lose the red hue when the food is withdrawn. So these fish should not be sold as ,,Red Discus". Most young fish from Asia are descended from Brown and Blue Discus. Heckels, too, are repeatedly crossed in. Unfortunately, good breeding specimens are rare, so that quality home-bred progeny are still valued highly abroad.

Brilliant Turquoise Discus in the romantic twilight of a densely planted-up display tank. The intensive colours show that the fish feel very much at home in a plant aquarium.

The Discus today

Today there are two kinds of Discus lover. The first group are those countless aquarists who generally purchase young specimens in the local pet shop because they like the look of the fish. They perhaps believe that young Discus are a worthwhile purchase because they are something special and will turn into fine fish in due course. They will no doubt have to tolerate some losses amongst their Discus if they keep them in a community tank. However, they will try again and perhaps even a third time. At some point they give up keeping Discus. A few will learn from their mistakes, go in for Discus more intensively and set up special Discus tanks. Then, undoubtedly, their efforts will one day prove successful and these aquarists will then join the second group, amongst whom I number the readers of this book – a not exactly small group of Discus lovers who have become devoted to this fish. Once infected by the Discus bacillus they can already be counted amongst those aquarists who know how to keep Discus successfully and perhaps even persuade them to breed.

Discus breeders who for various reasons have reached near professional standards in breeding remain a fringe group. But even here there are distinctions. Some of these breeders pursue their hobby because it is a challenge. The sale of successfully homebred fish raises just enough to cover their expenses. Perhaps now and again they earn a little from it, but when we include the work put in, the account drops back into the red. Professional breeders have already turned to massproduction, most of them trying to meet certain quality standards. These breeders generally sell their progeny to wholesalers, but sometimes to private people as well. The main object must, however, be the sale of whole broods, at the age of six weeks. Here, already, large-scale sales are required. Home-bred Discus are now sold in large quantities in Continental Europe, Britain and the USA.

Unfortunately, still far too few quality progeny reach the German wholesalers and retailers. A shortage persists, because quality specimens are required, which are healthy and stable. There is undoubtedly still a market here for Discus breeders. Small home-bred specimens 2–2,5 in. (3–6 cm) in legth are easily obtained. Medium-sized fish of 6 to 8 months are already harder to find, although they have every advantage. Here, the purchaser will already be able to judge the colouring, the body shape and the general appearance of the fish. And, of course, the price will still be worthwhile. If diligently kept, the purchaser will already have viable breeding specimens after a few months.

Mature adult specimens whith good or even very good colouring are very difficult to obtain. Even where such fish are advertised, the reality is rather different.

Discus fish are not easily raised. Because of their size, Discus fish already restrict the raising potential from an age of six months or so. These fish can be quarrelsome and aquariums containing a dozen of these yobs will already have its share of struggles for power and territory. If the fish are then still to be raised further, at least 8–13 gallons (30–50 litres) of water must be allowed for each fish. It will already be clear why so few adult fish appear on the market. What's more a hobbyist who has taken the time and trouble to raise good specimens will be unwilling to sell them again. Once he eventually has a dozen large Discus in his own tank, he will want to setup pairs and produce successful young Discus of his own.

Amongst Discus lovers, only quality specimens with good colouring can still be sold. The colour trend in recent years has clearly been towards the Turquoise Discus, striped speci-

A male Brilliant-Turquoise

mens being particularly favoured. Solid Turquoise Discus are rather less in quantity and are still the exeption. Also available are Red-turquoise Discus, though this calls for a word of warning. The composition of the water, e.g. the iron content, may influence the colouring of the fishes. It has been found that specimens with a pronounced red proportion in the basic colouring began to lose this in the new owner's tank, which was the result of the composition of the water.

Other hues play a subordinate role. Ordinary Brown or Green Discus are no longer saleable, or at least, aquarists have become so demanding that they still only want Turquoise specimens. Even beginners keep away from home-bred Browns, although it would be wise to more easily kept. An adult Brown Discus can be the centrepoint of an aquarium. Between green plants and large bogwood roots the fish is king.

The number of Discus lover is increasing all the time. The quality of our homebred fish must therefore remain the supreme aim for serious discus breeders. Home-bred specimens must retain the sturdy, thickset, round shape of the Discus. If the colour gradations have also been successfully reproduced to the previous quality, the wildcaught varieties can largely be ignored, as is the case with other animals such as e.g. the canary, the parakeet and the ornamental trout. This, all said and done, is protection of the species and preservation of the boitope by on-breeding.

German-bred Discus – a hallmark of Quality

The well-known American Discus breeder Jack Wattley often travels to Germany to visit discus-keeping friends. As a result of these visits he has on more than one occasion taken German-bred fish back with him to the USA. Discus bred in Germany are very popular world-wide. Today, many of these small Discus go to Belgium, Holland, Great Britain, the USA, Canada and even Japan.

In Germany, a number of Discus breeders began in the early eighties to raise Discus in large numbers. As a large potential of very nicely coloured fish was available, large numbers of quality young reached the hobbyist market. The Royal-Blue and Turquoise varieties soon led the field. These morphs especially the Turquoise, are now bred in volume so that it often seems more difficult to obtain good homebred Browns than young Turquoise.

As a result of years of purposeful breeding, Discus fish have acquired colours of an intensity not found in nature. Selective breeding, a service performed by our Discus pioneers, has achieved this standard. The real difficulty in present-day breeding is that parent fish used for this purpose have the colour but no longer the traditional round shape of the Discus. Elongated Discus are becoming more and more frequent. These fish are often affected by growth damage. However, damage of this kind is not inherited so that we can be certain that an impaired parent fish will not pass on these defects. The growth of small Discus is soon impaired beyond recovery if they are taken ill in the first months of their lives. The breeder must therefore pay particular attention, especially in the first six months, to the growing Discus. Provided Germany can maintain the existing standard of quality, there can be little doubt that the country produces the finest and best Discus fish.

At the age of barely six weeks there's no further stopping the little rascals. They are separated from their parents and now need feeding five to six times a day so they grow rapidly and, especially, uniformly. The spotlight already picks out patches of colour.

26

Is the Discus really a problem fish?

Why is the Discus regarded as a problem fish? Why do so many aquarists believe that it is something for specialists only? Why does the Discus have the reputation of being prone to disease? These and similar questions are quickly answered.

The Discus is a problem fish only because people say it is. So-called Discus specialists have steadily built up the myth of breeding difficulties and problems in keeping it. Discus fall ill only if they are kept wrongly and inattentively. The Discus is tougher and more longlived than most ,,ordinary" pet fishes.

Of course, there are rules to be observed when looking after Discus which ensure that the fish remain healthy and bright.

The most important instrument the keeper has at his disposal is the water. In nature, Discus fish live in extremely soft water. However, this water contains many humins which are of vital importance to the fish. On the other hand, if we put too many humins in our tank water it will turn brown and turbid, which detracts from the appearance of the fish. No Discus-lover will want to see his fish swimming in a thick, brown soup. It is therefore advisable to keep them in medium-hard water of approx. 10 to 15° general hardness. The hardness should be reduced for breeding, though peat extracts, trace elements and multi-vitamins will be added.

The pH value of the aquarium water also requires particular attention. For keeping purposes, all values between pH 6 and pH 7 will do. What must be avoided at all costs is a sudden change in the pH value by using acids. With only a minor error, using acids can have catastrophic consequences for the fish. The pH value may sink sharply, especially when the water is very soft. Slight corrections of the pH value may be made by filtering the water over peat.

A slightly acid environment should be aimed at for breeding. However, once again, the pH value should not fall below pH 5. Breeding water acidulated with peat also benefits the eggs laid. The bactericide effect of the peat is beyond doubt and prevents mould from forming on the eggs.

The Discus keeper must watch the water temperature particularly carefully. The Discus likes warm water. Ideal keeping temperatures are 84° – 86° F (29 to 30° C). Temperatures below 82° F (28° C) must be carefully avoided. If you want to do your fish a favour, the temperature may from time to time be raised slowly in the course of a day to 88° – 90° F (31 to 32° C), and then allowed to drop back to normal on the third day.

Changes in water temperature also stimulate egg-laying. The fish can be stimulated to courtship and egg-laying by a water-change, with water added to the tank which is rather colder or warmer than that present. This, of course, depends on the fish being ready for spawning.

As it is exremely difficult to protect fish against bacterial attack in small aquariums with a proportionately small volume of water, it must again be stressed that the best means of preventing this is a part water-change. If the tanks are overpopulated or if too little water is changed the nitrate and nitrite content in the water will necessarily rise. As stated, these toxins can be removed by changing the water or by installing ion-exchangers.

The exchanger resins regulate the pH value at the same time, adjusting it to a level of between pH 6 and 7. Make sure, however, that you use an exchanger resin which leaves the humins in the water.

Of course, whether a Discus feels at home depends greatly on the food it is given. As we shall largely be keeping only tank-bred specimens, we can forget about the eating habits of

Discus fish spawning

The series of pictures shows Discus fish spawning. A fine couple have teamed up in order to spawn. Both fish ar 16 months old and are descended from related lines. The male swimming on the left is rather more powerful in body build than the female.

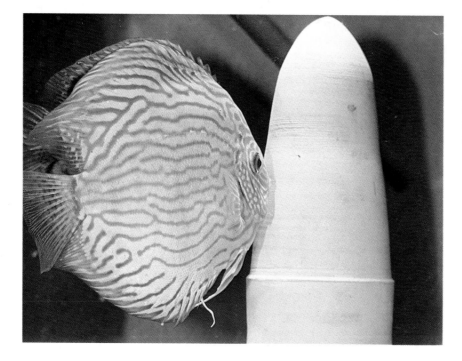

The male has accepted the pottery cone as a spawning place and starts cleaning the cone. This is a sure sign that spawning is imminent. The female also sits by the cone, concealed behind the male. Pairs in such close harmony can be expected to look after eggs and larvae well.

The female has donned her typical spawning dress. The last four or five stripes turn visibly darker as does the area around the tips of the ventral and dorsal fins. The expert refers to this as ,,sooting''.

Now egg-laying commences. String after string of eggs is laid. The pair are now fully engaged on their business. The male waits next to the female by the cone to fertilise the eggs deposited as soon as she moves away. Spawning takes up to an hour, after which both parents alternately guard the clutch.

the wild varieties. In nature, Discus fish prefer-ably feed off fresh water shrimps.

Variety is the key to feeding. It goes without saying that the fish must be offered a selection of various kinds of food. If fish are given one kind of food only it is hardly surprising that the female will not show a tendency to spawn. The stan-dard Discus foods include not only the dry varieties, for example Tetra Discus Food. But also, especially, beef hearts and enchytraea. When beef hearts and enchytraea are further enriched with vitamins and minerals there is little further they could wish for.

Many Discus are kept in aquariums without substrate and furnishings. However, there are some aquarists who prefer to see their Discus in planted-up and fully furnished tanks.

In tanks of this kind, the quality of the substrate and of the roots introduced must, especially, be kept under control. The substrate in particular conceals hazards. Food residues easily settle in the gravel or foul gases develop. Bogwood roots, too, may introduce decay in the water and start to smell unpleasant. The build-up of nitrite and nitrate then soon reaches a level which is harm-ful to the Discus. The fish turn dark and stick to one corner of the tank. It is now high time that the aquarist takes suitable steps. One solution, for example, is to cover part of the tank bottom with gravel. The glass bottom is left exposed in the front of the aquarium while a layer of gravel and aquarium plants is built-up at the back. Tanks of this kind are easily cleaned and still look good. If the Discus-lover observes these rules he will already have avoided many problems.

This Discus is showing dark body stripes, a typical sign of fright.

Keeping or Breeding?

This question must be at the fore-front of our minds when first acquiring Discus fish. True, most aquarists who acquire Discus will also have the particular desire to breed from the fish on occasion. The more so, since as with many cichlids, the brood care of the Discus is both interesting and delightful. Watching a broody Discus pair must be the greatest pleasure an aquarium-keeper can enjoy!

Let us first consider the idea of Discus-keeping. Care of the fish takes pride of place. Breeding has no part to play when contemplating purchase.

In principle, we must decide whether the fish are to be kept in a plant aquarium or in a Discus tank without further furnishings. In the former case, the plants must be selected with the Discus in mind.

When selecting the plants we must also remember that Discus can be kept only at temperatures above 82° F (28° C). You cannot make compromises here as Discus kept in water which is too cool will soon take ill.

It is by no means easy to reconcile plant and fish requirements in this case with a successful display aquarium as the end result.

Effective growth of water plants means a tank with a suitable substrate. As water plants must be properly provided with natural iron the bottom layer of sand should be mixed with an iron-containing substrate, for example Tetra Initial D. The installation of substrate cable heating should also be aimed at, so the plants do not get ,,cold roots", while a heated substrate also improves the circulation of the water. A natural flow of water is created along the bottom of the aquarium which benefits both plants and the continued stability of the substrate. The prepared sand layer is covered with a further layer of gravel, consisting only of washed stones. A harmonious picture is created for the observer if the gravel rises lightly towards the back of the tank. Discus fish, too, like shelters and markers when forming their territories. Stones are particularly suitable for this purpose though they should not make the water hard. Lava, granite and slate are suitable for this purpose. Particular caution is required with bogwood roots as they introduce yeasts to the water which can cause serious problems. In fact, many a ,,discus disease" in the community or plant aquarium can be cured simply by removing the roots present in the tank.

Excessively dense vegetation can easily have a negative effect. The fish hide amongst the plants, become timid and are lost from sight. Following a planting plan is therefore advisable whenever a new tank is set up. But do not forget that water plants grow and reproduce.

For the vegetation plan, a sketch must be prepared showing all the plant locations. In a Discus tank, the vegetation will necessarily look somewhat sparse to begin with, but as the plants grow appearances will already have improved within two months. There is no cutting corners whit the quality of water plants. Only true water plants must be purchased. A number of attractive plants are available through the trade which are well suited as bog plants for growing above water but once immersed they cease growing and soon perish. Plants with deep or varied colours should, in particular, be avoided.

The more important plants which have proved worthwhile in setting up a Discus tank are listed here for your guidance. Select species with a low height and which form ,,lawns" for foreground planting. Solitary individual specimens give the Discus tank the necessary depth without the fish being able to hide too much behind them. Tall, slender species are preferable for the background.

Aponogetons, or Sword Plants, are suitable for all Discus tanks as they tolerate temperatures of around 82° F (28° C). All species of Aponogetons have corms and need a period of rest. In the aquarium they grow for six months or so and then begin to contract. The corms must now be moved from the aquarium and kept for several months in a cool place in wet gravel or damp peat. After resting for two months, they are returned to the aquarium where they will again quickly grow into fine plants.

Aponogeton crispus – Ruffled Aponogeton

The narrow, lanceolate leaves are waved and slightly ruffled at the edge. The plants need plenty of light but then grow excellently. They readily flower in the aquarium.

Aponogeton henkelianus

This species of Aponogeton grows very easily and makes no demands. As a solitary specimen it is the centrepoint for every aquarium. It grows to 20 inches (50 cm).

Aponogeton ulvaceus

A tender, transparent plant, but still robust enough for the Disus tank. Its lush light green catches the eye. It can grow to more than 24 inches (60 cm) but generally stays smaller.

Aponogeton undulatus

This can be found in every pet fish shop. A fast-growing plant with strong, olive-green leaves. It is particularly suitable for background group planting.

Crinum natans crispus

A bulb plant with narrow darkgreen, knotted leaves, essentially curly and wavy. Owing to its extraordinarily shaped leaves it is an attractive display plant and also especially recommended for solitary planting. Because of its compact, leathery leaf structure your fish can do it little harm. In the aquarium it grows up to 20 inches (50 cm).

Crinum thaianum

A water-lily growing from a bulb. The species grows up to 40 inches (100 cm). Its long, band-like leaves then float on the surface where they form a natural cover. They should therefore always be planted towards the back and in corners.

Cryptocorynes with their strong, broad leaves fit well in the Discus tank where they proved ground cover. However, they should not be planted too densely as regular cleaning of the substrate will be difficult. All ,,crypts" grow very slowly and make specific demands on the quality of the substrate. They easily tolerate temperatures of 82° F (28° C).

Cryptocoryne affinis

A well-known species of crypt with a sturdy habit. The upper side of the leaf is dark green, the other side reddish. They produce many shoots and will quickly spread if they feel comfortable. As they grow to only 16 inches (15 cm) they are suitable as foreground plants.

Cryptocoryne balansae

This crypt has narrow, strongly knotted, greenish-brownish leaves. It needs plenty of

A display tank fitted out with an abundance of plants creates a magic garden for the observer. Healthy Discus feel particularly at ease and readily spawn in this biotope.

*In a tank which is open at the top, floating plants
provide welcome shelter for Discus.*

*The Kribensis (Pelvicachromis pulcher) remains small
and is a peaceful partner for Discus when kept together
in the plant aquarium.*

light but makes no other demands. It can grow
up to 16 inches (40 cm) and is suitable for
middleground planting.

Cryptocoryne ciliata

Under good lighting it grows up to 20 iches (50
cm). A fine solitary plant reproducing by
runners. A group of 3 to 4 plants at the back of the
tank is also to be recommended.

Cryptocoryne parva

A species of crypt which remains extremely
small. It grows to only 2 inches (5 cm) and is
therefore particularly suitable for foreground
planting to form a ,,carpet''. The fine, lanceolate
leaflets are sharply pointed. They grow very
slowly but steadily.

Echinodorus are Sword Plants. They are bog
plants from South America. Echinodorus species
are commonly found in the aquarium and
nearly all well suited to the Discus tank. Given a
nutrient-rich substrate they respond by good
growth. The family includes both tiny dwarf
plants for foreground planting and gigantic
display plants. The species listed here tolerate
water temperatures of up to 86° F
(30° C), which predestines them for our Discus
tank.

Echinodorus amazonicus – small leaved Amazonian Sword Plant

Light green, lanceolate leaves on short stems
are a feature of this plant. Placed in groups they
grow to 14 inches (35 cm). On their own they can
reach heights of 20 inches (50 cm).

Echinodorus cordifolius – Cellophane Plant

A majestic plant. The centrepoint for large
aquariums. It grows up to 20 inches (50 cm) and
has light green, roundish to heart-shaped leaves
which can achieve diameters of up to 8 inches

(20 cm). The plant tends to adapt to the size of the
aquarium. Strong-growing floating leaves must
be removed immediately.

Echinodorus muricatus – Horizontal Sword Plant

A sword plant similar to the Cellophane plant
but with tapering leaves. The light green leaves
are sometimes spotted brown. The plants grow
fast and reach 24 inches (60 cm), when they may
project from the edge of the aquarium. It then
forms an attractive display plant but the keeper
must be prepared for this eventuality.

Echinodorus paniculatus – Bleher's Sword plant

This is one of the best loved of the sword plants
and grows well. Its soft green, lanceolate leaves
grow to 3 inches (8 cm) across. Large solitary
plants form bushes with up to 50 leaves. Several
of these plants set in the background are the
right backdrop for a Discus tank.

Echinodorus grisebachii – Dwarf Amazon Sword Plant

Many aquarists will be familiar with this dwarf
sword plant. It forms a carpet in the foreground.
It grows to only 4 inches (10 cm). It sends out
runners which quickly form dense foreground
vegetation.

Echinodorus tenelleus – Junior Amazon Sword Plant

Growing to 2 inches (5 cm), this is a true dwarf
amongst the Amazon sword plants. It grows best
when given adequate light. With its runners it
forms a fine, dense carpet of green in the
aquarium.

Vallisneria are slender, decorative background plants which make no special demands
as to aquarium water. They also tolerate temperatures of up to 86° F (30° C).

Vallisneria gigantea – Giant Vallis

Growing up to 80 inches (200 cm), this plant does full honour to its name. The strap-type leaves grow to 1,5 inches (3 cm) across, turning over as they reach the surface. It sends out many runners and reproduces well. A decorative background plant if placed in groups of 3 to 5 specimens.

Vallisneria spiralis – Common Vallis

The light-green, strap-type leaves reach about ½ inch (1 cm) across. „Spiralis" because the flowering stems of the female plants grow in a spiral. It also sends out many runners and grows very strongly. This Vallisneria reaches 20 inches (50 cm).

Vesicularia dubyana – Java Moss

An aquarium moss which prospers well, covering stones and decorations with its dark green mossy carpet. It does not need a great deal of light.

The aquarium plants listed are a selection of ideal water plants for a Discus display tank. If the plants are to prosper, not only the substrate but other factors must be taken into account. Allowances must then also be made for the demands and living habits of the Discus fish.

As water plants come from the tropics they nearly all need plenty of light. 12 hours a day is the ideal period. Three fluorescent tubes are needed for a water depth of 20 inches (50 cm). Optimum reflection of the light is achieved by a reflector above the tubes, too much light otherwise being lost. We must also remember that fluorescent tubes lose up to half of their strength after six months.

An alternative to the fluorescent tube is the mercury vapour lamp. This is freely suspended above the aquarium, which must then no longer be covered. This means that the water plants can then grow out of the aquarium, so creating a quite special feature. When selecting the lighting and setting up the aquarium, some rather darker corners must be left for the fish to which a Discus can then retire. It is quite wrong to say that Discus like only dimly lit and dark aquariums. After all, in nature it is exposed fully to the tropical daylight.

Once the aquarium has been planted up for Discus it must be given an opportunity of running itself in. The aquarist must be generous in this case and allow at least a fortnight, or preferably four weeks, befor introducing his Discus to the tank. As algae are prone to emerge in a newly set-up plant aquarium, algae-eating

This pair shows successful breeding. But, unfortunately, the rules for ideal pair formation have been ignored. A splendid Brilliant-Turquoise male has been paired with a simple Green female. The eggs are already largely mildewed.

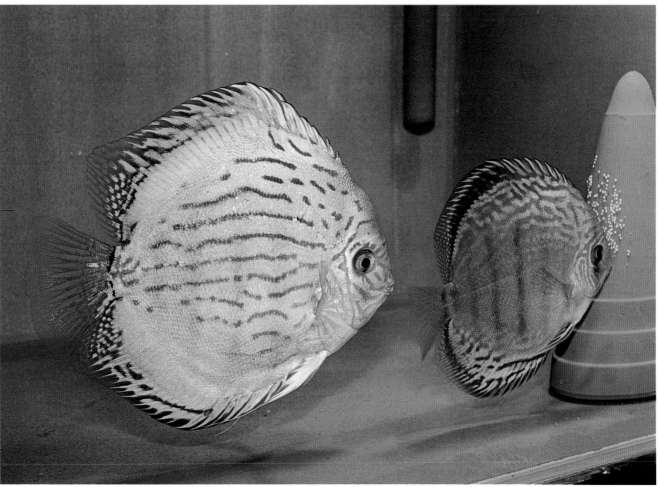

fishes should be installed from the start. From four to six Chinese Algae-eaters (Gyrinocheilus aymonieri) and three to five Otocinclus Catfishes are suitable for an aquarium holding 50 to 75 gallons (200 to 300 litres). However, these fishes should not be fed specially in the first two or three weeks so they can concentrate on devouring the algae. A few armoured catfishes can be introduced later to clear up food scraps.

Not many fishes settle down well with Discus. Whether a Discus display tank needs any ohter fishes at all should be carefully considered. Angels will certainly not do, as these predatory eaters snap up much of the food intended for the Discus and also introduce parasitic disease. If you really want to keep other fishes in company with your Discus you should concentrate on a shoal of Amazon fishes such as Glowlight Tetras, Pretty Tetras, Red-nosed Tetras, Rodway's Tetras, Ornate Tetras, Rosy-finned Tetras, Serpa Tetras or Neon Tetras. As all these Tetras are shoaling fishes and are seen at their best only in quantity, at least ten should be kept together in a group. In large tanks, a pair of Rams, which are of course particularly peaceful, can accompany the Discus. The centre-point of the tank, however, should always be the Discus themselves.

How many Discus can be kept in an aquarium of this kind? As it is a shoaling fish by nature, the Discus should never be kept on its own. If you would like to start with young fish, at least four but no more than eight should be kept in a 50–75 gallons (200 to 300 litre) aquarium. Just two adult Discus can also look very attractive. Should you have the good luck of purchasing a pair from a reputable dealer which get along well together you will have a first-class showpiece in your aquarium. A Discus pair in a plant aquarium of this kind is what every Discus-lover dreams of. It is also possible to breed Discus in a plant aquarium. True, you will not be able to raise a whole brood, as many young may perhaps fall victim to fellow inmates, but this natural environment together with the brood care by the parents makes up for a great deal.

When keeping the fish in this way you, as a Discus-lover, will have much pleasure. That the water quality of a plant tank of this kind must be kept under constant view of course goes without saying. The pH value should be kept below pH 7.0 as much as possible, which is also better for the plants. Different values can be tested with Tetra Laborett. With carbon dioxide fertilisation, which guarantees better plant growth, a check must also be kept on the nitrate content of the water as Discus react negatively to water which contains efussive nitrate.

Where the Discus-lover wishes to devote himself to breeding these fish, the position is immediately rather different. Breeding them requires a great deal of love and attention. Breeding Discus as a sideline usually ends in frustration. A Discus installation must have a purpose and an aim even before it is set up. The technical fitting up of an installation of this kind is described in a later chapter.

Breeding Discus requires a great deal of time. The serious breeder who does not breed for the sake of financial success must keep at least three or four aquariums to achieve his object. This quickly amounts to 125–250 gallons (500 to 1000 litres) of water which must be cared for daily. The time spent on cleaning the tank and filter, on feeding the fish and on part-water changing will already take up some two hours a day, even with smaller installations. Discus breeding can soon become a full-time job. One breeding tank is not enough to start with since a second pair will be desirable for selection purposes. As Discus fish may quarrel even when looking after the brood, an escape tank must be available. At

This Turquoise pair have formed a perfect couple as the two fish look almost identical, with similar inherited features. The offspring are also likely to be fine specimens.

least one larger tank must also be ready for the anticipated progeny.

If both couples raise the young, two raising tanks are already necessary. Since, however, Discus cannot be raised in large quantities in normal aquariums, the young must either quickly be sold or a start must be made on setting up yet a further aquarium. However, slowly but surely a quite remarkable Discus breeding installation is built up in this way.

The goal of Discus breeding should be to establish shades of colour and the typical Discus shape. This is not easy. Successful progeny all to quickly seduces the newcomer to Discus breeding into attempting to repeat his success without regard for the quality of the parent fish. As a result various morphs are crossed and young are obtained which do not comply with the racial characteristic. There is little use in crossing a good Turquoise Discus with a simple Brown Discus. The colour of most of the progeny will be unsatisfactory. These weakcoloured tank-bred specimens are very difficult to sell. A purchaser of Discus progeny expects good quality. This does not mean that Brown Discus are hard to dispose of. Good intensively brown-coloured Discus are bound to find a purchaser, the more so since these fish are now an exeption on the European market. If the traditional hues are bred in pure form they will always find a market. However, top prices will always be paid for a good Turquoise. If the breeder succeeds in producing quality fish in Brilliant Turquoise or Plain Turquoise, he will have no difficulty in finding willing purchasers for them.

Advice on buying Discus

Buying Discus is a matter of trust, and this needs some explanation. Discus fish are not mass-produced. True, every month several thousand young Discus fish are sold in Germany, yet when buying them certain basic rules must be observed. Discus should be bought where the purchaser can be sure that he receives the fish he is being offered. If he buys Turquoise offspring, Turquoise is what should be swimming in his tank a few months later. After all, there is no way of telling the colour of small Discus which are only six weeks old and 2 inches (5 centimetres) long.

It is always worthwhile catching one in a net and holding it up against the light. Take a good look at it! Even at this age, the colour of the scales will already tell you what morph you have. Even small Turquoise Discus must show an iridescent greenish colour. The true Turquoise sheen must be visible right across the body. Not simply the head colour but the whole body must be examined. This method also holds good for large fish. As lighting plays an important part in the brilliance of Discus colouring, the existing colours will be properly seen when the fish is removed from the water. In another tank, under better lighting, a previously unremarkable fish will display its full beauty. The time of day and the condition of the fish also plays a part. They are particulary good in the evening hours. The fish will also put on their full finery if they are healthy and feel at home.

Discus fish must be round. The body shape must already be visible in the young fish. Elongated Discus have stunted growth. This impairment is immediately evident in enlarged eyes. If the eye seems too large compared with the rest of the body, the fish has not grown properly. It must have been ill at some time and refused to take food for a while. This damage is already beyond repair. Even when very well kept, damaged fish will not grow back into shape. However, the defect is not inherited. All that mishapen Discus fish pass on to their progeny are their natural, inborn features. Damage caused by human hands during raising and keeping is not passed on to the young. If the progeny is looked after well, they will attain the ,,normal", sturdy Discus shape and differ quite clearly from that of their parents.

When buying young fish, particular care must be taken that they do not have ,,knife-edged" backs. Seen from the front or from above, the knife edge will be clearly visible. Young Discus whose head and back sections have receded in this way are beyond recovery and unsuited for subsequent breeding. Seen from the front and from above, the head section of a healthy Discus fish must be clearly rounded outwards, the shape of the head being round especially above the eyes.

Buying Discus takes time. An observer sitting quietly in front of a tank for several minutes will soon see what is wrong in it. Caution is necessary if the fish are timid and hide in a dark patch in the aquarium. Healthy Discus also show their vertical stripes as these signals are used when battling for territory. Visible vertical stripes show there is nothing wrong with the fish health. If, however, they are dark right across their bodies and the colour does not quickly return to normal, it is better not to buy them. Healthy Discus produce reddish-brown to black excrement, depending on the food. Large lumps of excre-

*From a shoal of Discusfish of the same age one could
with plenty of patience once with some experience find
a pair.
Here one could use possible sex characteristic's to make
a choice.*

ment in the water or hanging from the fish point to their health. Whitish, transparent and gelatinous strings of faeces indicate an infestation with parasites. These parasites can certainly be dealt with, but the new owner must know how to go about it. Newcomers to Discus-keeping would do better to try their luck elsewhere.

Many Discus fish have small holes around the head. Why this should be so is difficult to say. As hexamita have so far not been discovered in Discus, we must assume that they are the result of attacks by a spironucleus, an algal fungus or other causes. Small holes the size of a pinhead round the eyes may be regarded as harmless and normal; they are probably a sign of ageing though it is already found in yearlings. Larger crater-type holes, on the other hand, are more serious. Discus with large, unlovely holes may be suffering from hole-in-the-head disease. If white lumps or growths appear in the holes on the head, the fish should not be purchased.

A further point that requires the attention of a Discus purchaser are the gills of the fish. Discus suffer easily from gillworm and gill parasites. Fish infested with parasites or worms breathe on one side only. This means that only one gill cover is spread at a time for breathing. The second cover is held close to the head. Rubbing of the gills against items of aquarium furniture also indicates infestation. Gillworms or parasites are a nuisance; they make life hard for the Discus. The problem can be cleared up with medicaments but the new owner will have to spend some time treating the fish. This also presupposes that a quarantine tank is available as the fish must first spend two weeks in quarantine before they can be put together with other fishes already present.

As the purchase price for Discus is always relatively high, the purchaser may ask for them to be fed before his eyes. The well-being of adult specimens, in particular, which may easily cost several hundred Dollars must be checked in this way.

The fish should show interest in the food offered. They are peaceful eaters who like to take their time. If they are healthy they will select something from the food offered. However, they should not eat too much before a potential move as the water may then be polluted during the lengthy journey. They may disgorge food already taken when being caught.

The fish can be transported without oxygen over short distances. However, the amount of water must be adjusted to the length of the journey. The longer the journey, the more water must be used. The safest way of transporting them is in a plastic bag, placed in a carton. The cartons can be wellpadded with polystyrene or paper. Strong bags are available through the warehousing trade, where very good plastic bags are used for packaging cereals. Larger fish can simply make holes in plastic bags so at least two bags should be used, one inside the other. Never carry Discus directly in polystyrene boxes or plastic buckets. The fish are timid and may easily be injured against the hard walls. Damage to the membrane of the eyes can be acute in such cases. Once damaged, eyes usually stay that way. The pupil wastes away and remains small.

Peroxide tablets should not be used as, if given in the wrong quantities, they may prove detrimental to the mucous membrane of the fish. Pure oxygen from a bottle is ideal. With pure oxygen, the fish can happily withstand 36 hours in insulated polystyrene packs.

Transfer to the new home aquarium must be undertaken carefully. The tank water should be poured slowly into the carrier bag. The temperature and pH value should have adjusted within half an hour. The new fish can now be carefully

removed with a net. The carrying water should be thrown away.

At first, large Discus adapt very poorly to the aquarium. They sometimes even lie flat on the bottom. They breath very heavily and the eyes bulge from their sockets. This is no reason for major panic since within a hour the fish will already feel much happier in its new home.

The fish should not be fed during the first day. Small Discus, on the other hand, very quickly regain their appetites and should be fed soon after.

This healthy young Discus already displays its fine turquoise colouring at the age of ten weeks.

Selections of breeding stock

As it is the aim of nearly every Discus-lover to breed these fine fish, special attention must be paid to the quality of the breeding fish. Breeding must start out with good specimens. What is redquired is a good, high-backed shape and keen colours. The round, thickset discus shape, in particular, should be retained in the progeny. Crossing different morphs too strongly should be avoided. While it is true that inherited features are established by selective breeding, this presupposes that there is sufficient space for an adequate number of fish with the necessary features.

To start with, a number of young fish may be procured. Because of possible inbreeding, however, fish from more than one pair should be raised for subsequent breeding and the young of a second or third pair should be added in parallel. As it is not easy to raise young Discus without incurring some damage, sufficient young must also be kept available for this purpose. This means that the aquarist who seriously intends to build up his breeding stock should raise at least twenty and preferably thirty or forty young.

With the space normally available, it is of course difficult to raise forty Discus at a time. This is not essential but the greater the number of young available the more opportunity there is for selection. After four to six months the young will have grown to 2–3 inches (6–8 cm) and already display fine colours. The body shape, too, measured at the eye, and the body size must be carefully examined, with a view to determining their sex.

The time has now come for making a selection. Half the fish can be earmarked for further breeding. The selection criteria are the incipient colours, the body size and shape. Those who do not come up completely to expectations should be given away. When selecting specimens by body size, care should already be taken at this stage to ensure that in addition to the largest of the young an equal number of medium-sized young is also retained for further keeping. Experience shows that amongst siblings the females are rather smaller than the males. If only large specimens are retained, it might mean a surplus of males at a later date. The best specimens are therefore selected from the original thirty or forty. First attempts at spawning will already be made after one year. However, the fish must be placed in smaller groups of three or four for this purpose. The fish will not readily form breeding pairs if kept in groups of ten or over in the aquarium.

Excellent pairs can be formed from the best fish obtained in this way. When forming pairs, an attempt should of course be made to get specimens who both show the desired markings to breed. Unfortunately, it sometimes happens that „ideal" pairs will not tolerate each other and that breeding is impossible. Because of this, it is easy to see why a largish number of fish with similar markings should be kept. Only then is specialised breeding possible. Specialised breeding is different from ordinary breeding in that, in this case, particular attention is paid to establishing the colour and the pattern of markings. The appearance of the „brand" on the body, for example is important. Fish whose lines run as parallel as possible are put together in order to establish this marking in the progeny. Or the high red proportion in ventral or pectoral fins should be retained and strengthened. When selecting the colours, fish with particular depth of colour should be combined.

If a strongly blue-coloured plain Discus can be persuaded to breed, the young are bound for the most part to be similarly plain and powerfully blue. These features can be increased yet further by possible backcrossing.

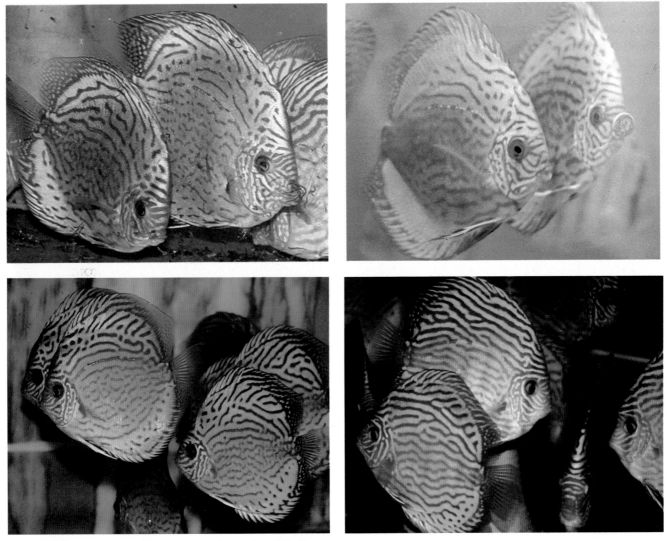

Strict selective breeding has allowed purebred Brilliant Turquoise, Red-turquoise and Striped Turquoise Discus to be bred. Maintaining this standard should be the aim.

A Discus breeder who wishes to apply himself seriously to specialised breeding and inbreeding in order to produce top class specimens must devote himself intensively to the theory of inheritance and put in a great amount of time. As the quality of Discus can be assessed only after they are several months old, selecting specimens for onward breeding is a time-consuming job.

The rewards of this arduous breeding work can be seen in the beautiful Discus fish swimming in hobbyists' tanks today. These fine fish have been developed from the natural forms. When comparing even the finest wild catches with Cobalts or Brilliant Turquoise, we must admit that such concentrations of colour simply do not occur in nature. Selection and specialised breeding for years on end have produced these results.

Nature has provided a fine Blue Discus – Symphysodon aequifasciatus haraldi. Man has selected a few of the finest from hundreds of these wild catches in order to breed Royal Blue Discus, Brilliant Discus and Cobalt Discus from them. Success has been achieved partly through mutations partly through stringent selection.

The Red Discus is now the dream of all breeders but this will still take some time to achieve. The base material exists but many factors play a part in this. It is unlikely that plain red specimens will be bred. Turquoise Discus with red cross stripes are already on the market. However, Turquoise with brownish-red stripes

Home-bred cross of Heckel's Discus and Royal Blue. The strong central stripe which is typical of Heckel's Discus is still pale in this case.

cannot as yet simply be offered as Red/Turquoise. Where this happens, it is usually more a case of wishful thinking by the breeder. The term "Red/Turquoise" should be used with special care. Perhaps a standard will be set one day for the Red/Turquoise, when this morph will become a component of the racial characteristic for the Discus fish.

Heredity for Discus Breeders

The Discus-lover will spend little time on the theory of heredity and the consequences of breeding Discus. If a pair forms in the tank or in the installation and it spawns, and diligently brings up its young, every owner will be happy. He would never dream of separating them merely for the sake of heredity. Nor is it necessary when they are bred as a hobby. Yet, some knowledge of the theory of heredity is necessary so we can understand the results of our efforts.

When breeding domestic pets and working animals, man uses his knowledge of the rules of heredity to breed-in certain features. Farmyard pigs became longer and leaner. They were bred with more ribs to obtain more chops. Japanese breeders have spent years breeding virtually boneless table carp. And Discus breeders, too, can influence their fish by resort to the rules of heredity. Inherited features are stored in the chromosomes.

The nucleus contains all the features of the parents. However, there are dominant features and recessive features. The dominant features persist and prevail over the recessive features which nonetheless remain stored. Amongst fish, the feature we look for, for example a strong turquoise colouring, is not dominant since fish in the wild are, as we know, less strikingly coloured as a protection against predators.

To bring Mendel's laws of heredity down to a common denominator, Turquoise Discus paired with a wild-caught Green Discus will produce offspring with the features of both though the "normal" wild form will predominate.

Since, however, the young possess the inherited features of both, their progeny will consist 50% of mixed breeds, 25% purebred Turquoise and 25% purebred Green Discus. Of the "grandchildren" of our first breeding pair, 25% now have the pure Turquoise features, the

A day-old Discus brood. The parents have rebedded the larvae from the spawning cone to the underside of a leaf.

remaining 75% look like the initial green wild-caught specimens. This colour feature can now be established with the pure Turquoise Discus by inbreeding. Of course, water quality and the behaviour and comfort of the fish play a role as far as the colour is concerned, but this does not affect the heredity. It is similarly impossible for fish fed with a particular coloured food to pass on this colour in any way. Deformations, scars from injuries and damage to the eyes through mishaps in transit are not, of course, inherited either. Even stunted growth in particular specimens is not pre-programmed in the inherited traits. Errors resulting through keeping will not affect heredity. Aquarist literature includes numerous scientific works on heredity,

On close inspection the segregations in the mucous membrane of the parent's skin are clearly visible.

most of which are very difficult to understand and not exactly easy reading.

Many Discus breeders who have been line-breeding or inbreeding with their Discus stock for a period of time have problems with their fish, especially as regards reducing size.

In line-breeding, fish of related Discus lines are paired. If lines whose forebears were distant relatives in the first degree are crossed, the valuable features of both lines can be preserved and established.

Inbreeding harbours certain risks. If fish from two different inbred strains are crossed after at least seven generations of inbreeding, large, fine, sensational Discus progeny may be the result. However, these fish will not unfortunately pass these features on to their young. Compared with the parents, the quality of the young will have deteriorated substantially. This method is based on the luxuriating growth of bastard forms

– known as heterosis. Heterosis will produce large Discus but beauty will go by the board.

To establish certain attractive features when breeding we must start with two related strains whose crosses produce very good results. The offspring of these crossed pairs may then be inbred with particular success over several generations. In practice, this means that Discus A of the first strain is paired with Discus B of the second strain. The offspring of this AB pairing may be inbred with each other. This means that the siblings amongst the offspring are crossed with each other. The ,,son" of A and B, therefore, with its ,,sister" of A and B. Inbreeding of this kind produces solid, satisfactory results. If the Discus breeder follows these rules he will have a fine, strong Discus breed in his tank for many years to come. The fish will look very much alike and there will be no difficulty in selling fish from an established strain of this kind. Hybrid breeding like this produces very pure strains of extremely similar fish. The serious breeder will then have reached his goal.

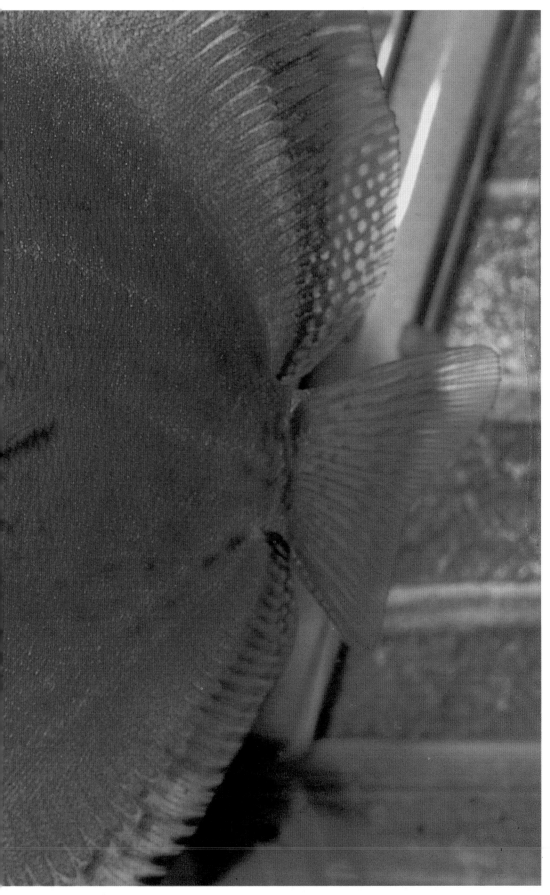

The eggs of this splendid Cobalt Turquoise Discus, while abundantly laid, unfortunately perished through poor water quality. A layer of mould can already be detected on the surface of the eggs.

Technical facilities
for keeping Discus

The aquarist industry offers all kinds of technical appliances for use in the aquarium. Thousand Dollars can soon be spent simply on equipment. Every serious Discus breeder will want to design his installation to his own requirements and there is no mould into which every Discus installation can simply be pressed.

A pre-requisite when planning is, of course, the water quality. Points such as desalination, nitrate removal, etc. must be settled.

Special tanks must be set up for breeding pairs. How large they should be is also a question of personal attitude and of space. Jack Wattley, for example, breeds his Discus fish in an aquarium containing less than 25 gallons (100 litres) of water. Often favoured are square aquaria 20 inches (50 cm) across, 20 inches (50 cm) tall and 20 inches (50 cm) deep. This provides a maximum of 30 gallons (125 litres) of water for each pair. A tank of this size could be regarded as normal, though they may be 24, 28, 32 inches (60, 70 or 80 cm) wide. Larger tanks are more complicated to maintain and it is also more difficult to feed fry in over-large tanks. The more water in a breeding tank, too, the easier the Artemia Nauplia distribute themselves, with the result that the young do not eat all the nauplia, leaving them to pollute the water.

Another argument against excessive breeding tanks is the higher energy requirement. As Discus fish are territorial spawners, i. e. delimit a specified territory for spawning, tanks containing 30 gallons (125 litres) are quite adequate.

Discus breeding tanks should not be placed too close to the floor. Ideal are shelves 32 to 40 inches (80 to 100 cm) up, on which the tanks are placed. As several breeding tanks are usually put together, the individual tanks should be screened off from each other. Poster board or cork tunnels will serve well. However, there must be enough space between the tanks for the screen to be removed when necessary. Discus fish need rest when they spawn. The screen should now be available so that the fish cannot be seen from the neighbouring tank. If the tanks are not screened, attempted scuffles might be the consequence, so that seminating males may be diverted too often and insemination prove inadequate. Much of the clutch would go mouldy.

As some Discus pairs also tend to eat their own eggs, removing the screen can work small wonders. Once the brooding fish see another Discus in the adjoining tank, their drive to protect their own eggs appears to be strengthened and they no longer attempt to eat them.

Other Discus pairs may quarrel fiercely after the eggs have been laid. Each wishes to guard the nest. Time and again, therefore, the pairs have to be separated, just one parent being left to look after the brood. Here, too, visible neighbouring fish may ensure that the parents do not fight, as they have then of course to deal first with the rivals in the adjoining aquarium. Many experiments can therefore be successfully concluded with screens between the tanks.

Each breeding tank should be operated as a self-contained unit. If every tank has its own filter there is no risk of disease being transferred. If eggs in a breeding tank are within a closed installation they may, for example, suffer when the water is changed in an adjoining tank. Foam plastic cartridge filters, e. g. Tetra Brillant Filter, are ideal for the breeding tank. No fry or larvae can be drawn into the cartridges. However, when the small Discus have grown a little and are no longer so dependent on their parents, a few inches (centimetres) of space should be left between the plastic and the aquarium wall as the young may otherwise become jammed between them.

The author in front of one of his breeding tanks. This Brilliant Turquoise female will take food from the hand and is very trusting.

These simple filter sytems suffice with regular water changing. They are operated by air so that a strong air pump (Tetra Luft Pump) will have to be purchased, as the installation will tend to grow rather than shrink.

There are a great many filtration methods which are suitable for keeping Discus. Large external filters have proved worthwhile. Many hobbyists have linked whole batteries of Discus tanks in their basements to one large external filter. The filter chambers for installations of this kind are run with rotary pumps which are suspended directly on the clear water chamber in the filter. From here, the water is pumped into a ring delivery pipe, the water being supplied to each tank through a special valve. The foul water is conveyed to the filter from the tank by over-pressure through a long overflow pipe.

Precise instructions appear in the book ,,Successful Discus Keeping." Larger individual tanks intended for raising young fish or for keeping several large specimens can be run with fast-acting internal filters. However, even here external filters have proved better. Fast rotary pumps filter the purified water from the clear water chamber directly to the tank. Foul water is removed from the tank through a simple overflow pipe and taken to the filter. Small external filters should have a large filter chamber and a smaller clear water chamber. The filter chamber may contain filter wadding, aquarium gravel, nitrate anion exchanger resin and two layers of plastic foam in sequence from bottom to top. Filter chambers of this kind can be run for several months without any problem. The exchanger resins can be re-used after regeneration and the wadding and gravel immediately after washing out. The foam plastic mats are used for coarse filtration and are rinsed out weekly.

As to the minimum size of such a filter, a rule of thumb is 10% of the volume of the tank.

As there are no water plants to clean and stabilise the water in a Discus installation, the aquarist must pay particular attention to water quality. For a Discus breeding installation this necessarily includes a good conductivity meter and a pH measurement gauge. The pH value in particular must be checked regularly as very soft aquarium water is very unstable and may quickly lose balance. Soft water tends to rise into the basic areas of 7.5 to 8.0 pH. Strong water movement through the filter or diffuser will release much of the captive CO_2 (carbon dioxide) and this will escape from the water. The pH value rises from the acid to the basic range. This should be avoided while breeding.

As soft water and high water temperatures are two factors which negatively influence the quality of the water, it is worth adopting a control medium. Two possibilities are ozone and ultraviolet radiation. UV radiation tubes can be linked straight into the filter system. An UV tube has a working life of some 7500 hours of continous operation. This means that the tubes must be replaced after 300 days at the latest, as their output is then no longer adequate. The task of the UV light is to kill germs in the water as they pass across the beams of light.

Ozone, too, has a germicide effect. No medicaments may be used during ozonisation. In addition, ozone attacks the nutrient mucus on the fish skin. Ozone should therefore be applied only until the Discus fish begin to secrete the mucus for their young. This means that the ozone system must be switched off by no later than the second day after the eggs have been laid.

Also important for healthy Discus fish is a part-water change. As Discus are bred and also generally kept in tanks without substrate the bottom of the tank must be regularly cleaned.

Discus produce large quantities of excrement as they are, of course, large fish. It is therefore advisable simply to vacuum off a full bucket of tank water with the soil every day or two. Firstly, therefore, the soil is removed and, secondly, a supply of good water is ensured. Adding Tetra AquaSafe to ensure new water is free of toxic chemicals, and Tetra Blackwater Extract to create an Amazon Basin environment are essential for Discus aquariums.

A quality heater and quality thermometer are absolutely necessary for any Discus aquarium. Your dealer can recommend the brand . . . but you should make sure it is the best.

Of course, Discus tanks must also be lighted. Not only the traditional fluorescent tubes but mercury vapour lamps and metal halide spots are now also available for fish-keeping. Only the fluorescent tube is suitable for fish-keeping and breeding installations. As there are no plants, the light intensity need not be inordinately high. As a rule, one fluorescent light above each tank suffices. The shade of colour used by the aquarist depends rather on individual taste. Natural light and Grolux tubes are available as well as the Warm-white types. The warm colour of the Grolux tubes is very popular amongst Discus keepers.

The neon tube is suspended some 8–12 inches (20 to 30 cm) above the water level so that it does not get in the way of work on the tank. The light yield can be increased by inserting an internal reflector to the fitting.

The young of the Discus also feel very much at home in a well set up plant tank. The water quality must be kept under consistent watch to prevent diseases.

Water Treatment

The „normal aquarist" is fortunate since when keeping fresh water fishes he need worry little about water treatment. This, however, is a chore no Discus-lover or breeder can escape.

First of all, the pH value of the water must be regularly checked as soft water is very unstable. The pH value measured shows the position with the hydrogen ion composition. The pH value scale ranges from pH 0.0 to pH 14.0. Water with a pH value of 7.0 is neutral. If the pH value falls, the water is on the „acid" side, if it rises, it will be on the basic or „alkaline" side. Discus feel happiest in a water with pH values of between 6.0 and 7.0. For breeding purposes, the pH value should be closer to values around 6.0 as this prevents mould from gathering on the eggs.

The pH value is most easily regulated by using exchanger resins or by adding aquarium peat.

As the pH value is important to the appetite and contentment of the fish and in persuading them to reproduce, it must be regularly checked.

It is certainly worth purchasing a measuring appliance. The electrode on the appliance is dipped in the aquarium water. The electrode produces an electrical voltage which is displayed on the appliance through an amplifier. Precise measurements are possible within seconds.

With continuous measurement the electrode can be kept permanently in the water. The measurement fluid in the glass container does not then diffuse so quickly. Fastened down with a suction cap measurements can be quickly taken.

Secondly, there is the conductivity of the water. All water contains dissolved substances, salts in particular. These salt ions conduct the current. The higher the ion concentration in the water, the more conductive it becomes. The conductance of saline sea water is very high, as is the conductivity of the water.

The conductance of the home waters of the Discus is very low. It is generally less than 50 μS (microsiemens). This indicates a water hardness of approx. 1° general hardness. There is then virtually no carbonate hardness in the water.

These factors must logically be taken into account when breeding as well. The breeding water must be made right for Discus. In many cases this means desalination. The osmotic pressure of the salt on the Discus egg can be reduced in this way. Under high pressure, the Discus eggs will otherwise be destroyed and gather mould. The destruction is generally invisible to the human eye. The eggs remain clear but no larvae develop. The internal pressure of the egg has prevented any onward development. The aquarist is happy because he can see clear eggs but days pass without their developing further.

The conductance of the breeding water should in no event be more than 300 μS, the carbonate hardness comprising the lesser part of the water hardness. The mains water in Germany, for example, is often very hard and unsuitable for breeding. It must therefore be softened or desalinated. Industrially produced ions exchanger resins are available for this purpose. These are microscopic granules of artificial resin and have long been used on industrial water treatment. In chemical terms, large quantities of cations or anions are bound to these granules. By exchanging the salts dissolved in the water with the ions the water quality is guided in certain directions. The dissolved salts can also be removed entirely from the water. These processes are known as decarbonisation, softening or desalination.

Water softening is particularly important for Discus breeders as hard mains water can be treated to suit the fish. Cation exchangers remove the existing carbonate. Calcium and

These two-week-old fry are still closely tied to their parents. They leave the parents only in search of further food.

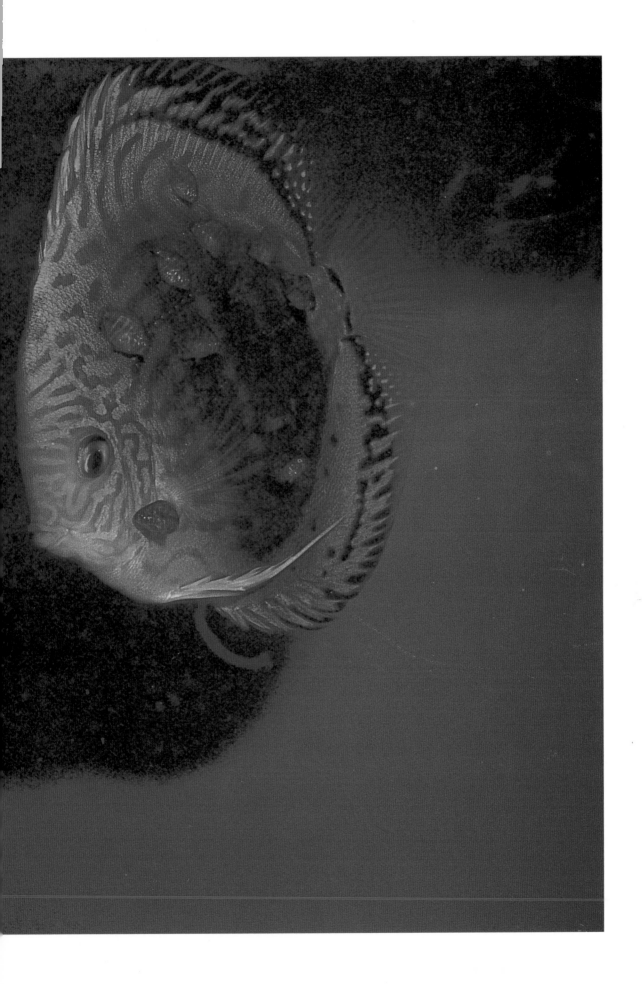

A splendid specimen of a Cobalt-striped Turquoise in its true, natural colouring.

magnesium are taken out of the water and replaced with sodium. The softening filters work very slowly. Special desalination filter columns are commercially available. They can be either integrated directly in the filter system or used as a bypass. Under the bypass system, a proportion of the filter water is passed across the resin through a hose system. The treated water is then returned to the filter chamber.

Softening resins are easily and safely regenerated with kitchen salt. Precise instructions for resins are delivered with the equipment. The sodium hydrocarbide produced by the carbonate hardness unfortunately renders the water alkaline. The pH value will fluctuate between pH 8.0 and 9.0. These values are of course undesirable for Discus. The water must therefore again be buffered with acids into safer pH areas.

The pH value must also be carefully controlled with decarbonisation, where only the carbonate hardness is removed. The carbonate hardness can be eliminated outside the aquarium by the filtration process relatively easily. The resin is regenerated with diluted hydrochloric acid. Necessary caution is of course required her, especially as regards the rinsing of the resins after regeneration. Careless use can all too easily produce a pH collapse in the tank, and the fish will die.

A further possibility is to desalinate the water. Something close to distilled water can be produced by a twin-filter process or a mixing bed outside the aquarium. The twin filter process is simpler to operate and less complex. In the first filter water passes through a cation exchanger regenerated with acids. In the second filter it passes through an anion exchanger. The water obtained in this way must be adjusted with other desalinated water or mains water. Fully desalinated water would the tantamount to keeping Discus in distilled water. Many aquarists have to desalinate their mains water and then have a salt deficient water, the important salts also unfortunately being removed by this process. Concentrations of the minerals and vitamins obtainable through the trade must then be added. Humins from aquarium peat must then also be applied (Blackwater Ectract). Only then will the water again be ,,live", but without containing the harmful salts.

This desalinated and retreated water must of course be checked for the right pH value and if necessary adjusted with acids or caustic soda solution.

The three methods described so far for treating water are all external ones. There are also internal methods of water treatment for maintaining water quality in the tank.

An ion exchanger resin conditioned with sodium hydrocarbide will ensure the pH value is maintained. The carbonate hardness is kept very low and the pH value will settle down at between pH 5.7 and 7.0.

It is, on the other hand, very important for the Discus keeper that metabolic products are removed together with the nitrates. As our installations will not include aquatic nitrate-consuming plants in any quantity, the harmful nitrate must again be eliminated by more frequent part-water changing or nitrate filtration. An anion exchanger in chloride form which can be installed like filter charcoal has proved useful for this purpose. This means that the resin is used as a post-filtration material in the external filter or a canister filter. Wadding, gravel or a similar material is used for pre-filtration. One litre of exchanger resin should be used for every 20 gallons (100 litres) of tank volume, so that, with a normal complement of fish, a working life is

achieved for the filter of 3 to 6 months. The resin is then reactivated with kitchen salt solution. A very simple and safe method.

The anion exchanger binds hydrogen carbonate and so also slightly reduces the carbonate hardness. In addition, the pH value is buffered in the pH 5.7 to 7.0 range, which is ideal for Discus. With this resin, the nitrate content is kept practically at zero for months at a time. This especially favours the growth of the young.

As the valuable humic acids, e. g. from aquarium peat, should be retained in the Discus tank, care must be taken when using this resin that the type purchased will allow the humins to be retained in the water. A version is in fact commercially available which removes the humins without trace and is of no use for Discus-keeping.

The application of these exchanger resins makes both the keeping and breeding of Discus much easier. There is a proviso, however, that the keeper is fully familiar with the systems.

It is particularly important that nitrates should be removed from water in which Discus are bred, successful breeders swearing by a maximum nitrate value of 0.15 mg per litre of water.

The rather smaller female of this Turquoise pair is almost plain. The inherited features of the fish were so outstanding that all progeny have the same intensity of colour.

Preparing for Breeding

A pre-requisite for successful discus breeding is a pair of suitable breeding fish. The Discus-lover who has the time can compose his first pairs from the young he has raised. Others must buy adult fish before they can start breeding.

Important for the composition of the pairs is to know their sex. It is a fact that there are no sure external characteristics for determining the sex and one can only go by assumptions. However, in the course of time the breeder will gain a sixth sense, both in sexing his fish and also when buying the fish he needs from other breeders.

What characteristics can we use to determine the sex? First of all, there is the general appearance of the fish. With fish of the same age, the males are generally more thickset and rather larger. Especially when viewed from the front, the males have broader and outwardly more strongly rounded skulls. The dorsal fins of male specimens generally come to a longer point and tend to curve upwards. Females have rather more rounded ends to their dorsal fins. The tailfin of the male Discus may appear rather broader than that of the female.

The two pennants may also be longer and broader in the male, though this characteristic should be evaluated with caution.

Powerful skulls, thick lips and a marked dewlap are commonly ascribed to males, though large females may also, of course, display these features. Behaviour in the tank is often also an indication.

However, the leader of the shoal may be either a male or a female. Generally speaking, when two fish are kept together in a tank, the male will set the pace. A pair will not normally tug at each others' mouths. The male will lightly dig the female in the side. He swims rapidly towards her, then suddenly turns away. The female usually displays her dark stripes clearly. If the fish are compatible and if the presumed male allows his partner to feed with him untroubled, they are certainly a pair. If, on the other hand, one of the fish hides in a corner of the aquarium when food is given, the two fish will be of the same sex.

Well-proven is the method of placing two fish which form a presumed pair in a tank. After a few days there can be little further doubt as to the sexes. If the two quarrel heavily they must be separated. When forming a new pair, the males should always be placed with the female already in the tank. The transferred male must then first get his bearings and cannot imme diately dash at the physically inferior female. If, on the other hand, Discus females are put with a male already in the tank, they are soon violently embraced and spend several days hiding in corners and at the water surface.

Once two suitable Discus have found each other in this way there will be a chance of successful progeny.

Apart from optimum breeding specimens, the technical facilities and the water quality must also be adjusted to breeding. The water should not only be prepared as mentioned but enriched with peat extract. For this purpose, aquarium peat can be mixed with water in a separate tank or in a plastic container. Aerated through a stone, the peat will then add humins and acids to the water. A proportion of this old water can be conveyed to the breeding tank after a few days. The fish will generally react positively to the slight change in the pH value and to the new composition of the water and possibly be stimulated to spawn. This is precisely the phenomenon which occurs in nature when new water is added during the rainy season. The peat can be bundled in gauze bags or a nylon stocking so it does not spread in the container. Another possibility would be to turn off the aeration system for

The parent fish still tries to keep the larvae in a shoal. The fry will very soon swim freely and then live off the skin secretion.

a few hours so the peat sudge can settle on the bottom of the container.

Ceramic vases have proved ideal as a spawning substrate for the eggs. However, Discus will also spawn on other articles. The spawning substrate should not have too smooth a surface which is why ceramic pots have proved very useful. Even ordinary clay flowerpots can be used, but the hole in the pot should be closed up as the fry may otherwise swim into it. In addition, sludge suspended in the water may also collect in it.

The right location for the breeding tank is also a criterion for the breeder. Discus fish like spawning in peace. Discus breeding facilities are often set up in basement rooms where the fish are unlikely to be disturbed, especially if the keeper only enters the room a few times. The fish panic and attempt to flee on a sudden disturbance or too much movement in the room. It has been proved that fish will become used to noise, disturbance and movement in front of the tank. The more disturbance regularly occurs, the less timid the fish will be. On bathing beaches with many bathers in the water, fish swim quite happily amongst the bathers without thinking of flight. Animals in zoos or wild-life parks are not frightened of people as they are used to seeing them. The position it the same with fish. Fish will become more timid the lower the tank is to the floor. If they are healthy, Discus will swim to the glass out of curiosity when a visitor stands in front of the aquarium. In fact, they should even be willing to take food from the hand. Discus get used to people and know precisely when it is feeding time and will then swim up towards them. This is another of the joys of keeping Discus.

Harmony and compatibility of the breeding pair is a prerequisite for successful breeding. Especially when feeding his fish will the breeder notice whether or not they get on with each other. If they fight fiercely for the food or it the male prevents his female from eating, there is little in the way of harmony.

Depending on the angle of the light these Turquoise Discus will show a greater or lesser amount of red in the cross-stripes.

Modern Discus installation for keeping and sale.

Successful Discus breeding

Successfully breeding Discus is the declared aim of many fresh water aquarists. A rewarding goal, if the principles set out in this book are observed when selecting the breeding pair. The interesting brood care of the Discus, which long remained unknown, is adequate compensation for a great deal of trouble. Does the hobby have anything finer to offer than the sacrificing brood care of two compatible parent fish? They look after the eggs and fan them tirelessly, subsequently releasing the larvae lovingly from the eggs and re-bedding them. When the fry swim freely, they make sure than none is lost. Time and again they swim off after the small larvae to bring them back to the fold. When, eventually, the fry swim freely, the parent fish offer them their skin secretion and allow themselves to be browsed indefatigably by a host of tiny mouths. The parent fish care for their young like this for weeks on end, until they have become independent. These weeks are probably the finest for the owner, who will continuously rush to his aquarium to see his splendid brood.

But, until that point is reached, the fish must first begin by spawning. When a Discus pair have found each other, they are bound to spawn soon. The process may greatly try their owner's patience. It may take weeks or even months until compatible fish also spawn. They are already sexually mature when barely one year old. Discus will spawn really effectively within an age of one to three years.

It is said of Discus that they start to spawn during periods of low atmospheric pressure. However, this hypothesis is not the only one in circulation. The females can produce a clutch of eggs weekly for week at a time during a spawning phase. One Discus female can deposit up to 20 clutches in this way within six months. Normally, of course, the female will look after its brood and then spawn again only when the fry

are taken from the tank. However, this repeated egg-laying has been observed of notorious eggeaters. Between the spawning phases the fish may have rest periods of several months. It may happen, therefore, that good pairs will suddenly make no further attempts to spawn for months, and then as suddenly start up again. When Discus start spawning can be see first of all from their colour change. The rear part of the body, in particular, turns darker. The last four stripes become visible and the tailfin looks sooty. The fish also begin to darken all along their bodies, which indicates that spawning is imminent.

The fish stand peacefully at the spawning cone. Now and then a shiver passes through their bodies. This is particulary noticeable at the head end. The fish fins quiver and they swim at each other. A nodding motion can also be observed.

The female now swims repeatedly to the ceramic cone and appears to spawn. However, she is not yet ready. Again and again, both partners clean the spawning substrate. The fish suck dirt off the cone, butting it hard. This cleaning process is a sure sign that spawning is imminent.

The female's ovipositor now becomes visible. This broad tube projects 3 to 4 millimeters from the body. The male's generative organ is shorter and comes to a point.

The female repeatedly starts test-spawning. The male is just an interested bystander. That is why other aquariums should be masked off, so the fish are not diverted. Of course, the timeswitch may not suddenly dowse the light at this point. The process will otherwise be broken off.

After the preparations for spawning, which may take a whole day, actual spawning commences. Discus spawn preferably during the evening. The female swims towards the spawn-

Discus female laying her eggs. The extended ovipositor can be clearly seen. The male stands by, ready to fertilise the eggs.

ing cone from beneath and lays one egg after the other on her way up. She will untiringly deposit an average of ten to twenty eggs in rows. The average clutch contains 200 eggs, good clutches some 300 eggs and top clutches 400 to 500. After every successive depositing the female makes room for the male, so he can immediately fertilise the eggs. There should at this point be no rapid current in the breeding tank. The filter must be throttled down.

A spawning session takes about one hour. The fish can be observed though they must not be disturbed. The sex can now be determined with absolute certainty and now and again presumed females may prove to be male. It is also important to see whether the fishes tolerate each other well. The better a Discus pair gets on, the greater the chances of survival for the fry. If the young fish can consistently choose between the skin secretion of both parents, their stomachs will always be full and they will grow faster in the first days.

After the eggs have been laid, the parents position themselves in front of the clutch and fan them with their pectorals. Harmonious pairs will relieve each other at regular intervals. If the parents already begin to squabble, the situation may become critical. If the squabbles get worse, the parents will probably eat the eggs as a result. Removing one of the fish may not even help. The fish left behind will promptly make for the eggs. However, even single fish can successfully raise young.

It repeatedly happens that Discus eat the hatched larvae. A solution in this case, too, can be to remove one fish from the breeding tank. A wet-nurse is even a possibility if the conditions are right. If another Discus pair has young at much the same time the fry can be removed from the tank with quarrelsome parents and slipped into the shoal of other young. The ,,new" parents

Discus larvae immediately after swimming free. These are the first, critical days, as the larvae then eat only skin secretion.

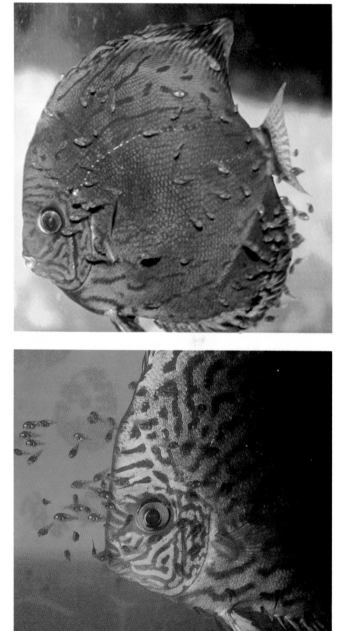

will not usually notice and will readily accept the additional fry. The eggs can also be taken from egg-eating parents in the same way, left to hatch artificially and the larvae then be smuggled in with another broody pair. Valuable young of poor parents can then be raised naturally.

However, let us go back to the egg-laying in the breeding tank. The eggs need some 60 hours at a temperature of 86° F (30° C) to develop. By the second day, dark spots inside the eggs are already visible to the naked eye. After 48 hours small eyes can even be seen.

The attentive parents help as soon as the larvae begin to hatch from the eggs. They simply "chew" the larvae out. The small larvae hang jerkingly with their vibrating tails to the spawning substrate. Adhesive glands in the head prevent them from falling off. This stage ends after a further 60 hours, when the fry begin to swim free. The parents will often re-bed the young at the larval stage. The larvae are settled at a different spot from that where the eggs adhered. Many a Discus-lover has sought his young charges in vain the next day, only suddenly to rediscover them later. The parents had simply re-bedded them.

During this stage of development from egg to free-swimming small Discus, a nightlight should be left burning near to the tank so the parents have time to gather up the fry in the evening and look after them overnight.

During this time the parents eat less but should still be regularly fed. Live food should be avoided as this confuses the fish. They must then distinguish between the young and the live mosquito larvae, which they find difficult to do.

It is important that the young should swim towards the parent fish as soon as they swim free. If they do not do so, they are lost. This happens quite often and the reason for it is not known. It is also possible that the parents do not

A mood photo of an exeptional Discus mother. The male had to be removed from the breeding tank as he was becoming intolerable. The female raised the numerous brood entirely on her own. Incompatibilities between the parents may endanger a whole, valuable brood.

*Head study of a striking Turquoise female. A strong red
eye in fascinating colour contrast to the powerful turquoise
blue of the body. Spotlighted from above, the colour
shading of a perfectly coloured Discus is evident. Specially
bred specimens of this quality are the result of long
selection, strict line breeding and inbreeding.*

Properly fertilised Discus eggs after approx. 48 hours. The embryos clearly stand out against the background of the spawning cone. The hatched Discus larvae continue to stay close together.

develop the skin secretion. in which case the brood is similarly lost. The young who swim towards the parents remain almost constantly in contact with their skin and eat the secretion almost uninterruptedly. At this period the parents also adopt a particularly dark colour.

For the first few days, the young will feed exclusively off the parents' skin secretion. Without the secretion, survival is not possible by natural means. Some breeders have tried, with a great deal of trouble and greater or lesser success, to raise Discus artificially. Wether artificial raising is to be aimed at need not concern us here. Were it to become the rule, it would soon mean an end to the Discus, as it would then have to follow the same road as the Angel. It would still be bred only for financial gain and young specimens would flood the market. Breeders looking for quality would

The male on the right is passing the
brood to the female. This ideal case of a
harmonious pair is the dream of every
breeder.

breed smaller numbers, if any at all. The result would be a collapse of quality standards.

The skin secretion is vital to the young for at least the first four or five days as they will eat no other food. Only then can the breeder start topping up their food with artemia shrimps.

While the young will initially always stay with the parents, they make for the artemia as soon as it is fed. In these first days they will venture as much as 2–3 inches (7 centimetres) away from the parents. As they grow older, the bond with the parents weakens.

It is interesting to note how the parents change roles while feeding the brood. Generally, one fish swims with the young while the other keeps an eye open for food in the tank or guards the territory.

A Discus pair will raise young even in the presence of other large specimens. The other inmates will keep well clear of a couple with young. The pair and their young will take over at least half of the aquarium.

The small fish will feed off the parents' secretion for two weeks altogether. The period may be extended by a day or two but by then the young have reached such a size that they may damage the parents' mucous membranes. The time has then come to seperate the fry.

After the fry have eaten their first artemia nauplia they will increasingly go for this food. To start with, the breeder will blow the nauplia directly into the shoal of young near the parents with a glass pipette. Later on, the small Discus will search the whole tank for these shrimps. Within a fortnight, the small fish will also greedily take fine flake, rubbed down Discus food and tablet food.

Raising the Young

Discus breeding and raising the young Discus are two quite different things. Once he has succeeded in breeding Discus fish, every breeder is faced with the problem of raising the young successfully. Raising can mean that he keeps the fish for six to eight weeks and then sells them. However, it can also mean keeping them until they reach adulthood, which entails caring for them for nine to twelve months.

As small Discus are generally sold at the age of eight weeks or so, it is important for them to be kept healthy during this period. To do so, regular part-water changing is important. One way of avoiding the risk of a rise in nitrate is to fit a nitrate filter to the raising tank. Discus young kept in excessive nitrate will show poor growth.

As these fish need feeding several times a day, their metabolic output is correspondingly high. The water is burdened with an above-average quantity of waste products. That is why the partial daily water change, with the impurities being vacuumed off, is so important. As fish generally grow better in harder, i. e. in mineral-rich water, mains water can safely be used for raising the young. Up to 20° of general hardness are acceptable in this case. The harder water is also far more stable as regards pH value. The risk of the pH values suddenly falling or rising sharply is then more remote.

Attention must remain focused on good water quality at all times. If fed well and adequately, the young fish will then grow rapidly. The first will already have reached the size of an 50-pence piece after six weeks.

Damage to the gill covers is a recurring problem with young Discus. There is still no hard and fast explanation for the cause. There are two theories. Firstly, in an over-small aquarium and with poor water quality, the oxygen supply may be insufficient for the young fish. They then stand in the tank, panting wildly. This may distort the gill covers. If the water quality is poor, inflammation of the gills may then be an added symptom.

The second theory is a deficiency in minerals and vitamins for the young fish. This is perfectly possible, since in the first three weeks of their lives the fish generally eat only artemia apart from the skin secretion. Vitamin concentrates should always be added to the artemia cultures. One drop of multi-vitamin solution should be supplied for each newly started culture bottled after 20 hours, when the artemia begin to hatch. The addition of a mineral product enough to cover a knife-tip might also help.

An almost solid Brilliant Turquoise with incipient
spawning colour. The edge of the dorsal fin is already
very dark. A fine contrast with the fish's powerful blue is
the luminous red eye.

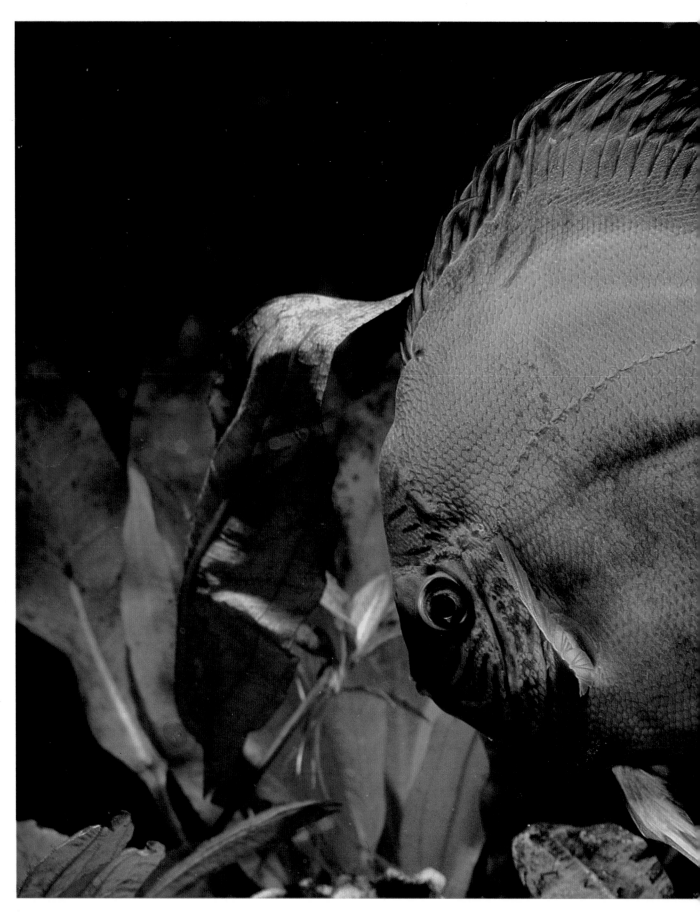

Professional Feeding

The majestic large Discus fish also have a king's appetite. They glide slowly towards the food offered, to suck it up daintily. They take their time and eat very slowly. Quite the opposite of the Angel, which darts quickly at any kind of food, the Discus is far more choosey.

In the wild, Discus fishes have to live chiefly on day-flies and their larvae or small fresh water shrimps (Macrobrachium).

To what extent Discus also eat largish quantities of algae has not yet been adequately researched.

Given time, Discus fish can be acclimated to a quite specific food. Any Discus can therefore quite easily be acclimated to TetraMin flake food. However, Tetra has developed a special Discus food – a slowly sinking food bit – ideal for its nutritional value and the fact Discus can feed in mid-water where they are most comfortable. A wild catch will not, of course, eat in its new owner's tank fon the first day. However, when accompanied with other flake or Discus Food eating Discus, the wild catch will eat after only a few days. It is, of course, much easier to get new fish to eat when they are kept together with domesticated fishes. The need for food is deep-felt and soon ensures that all fishes eat. Discus who leave the shoal while being fed are undoubtedly sick.

What other foods are suitable for large Discus? In addition to TetraMin flake and Tetra Discus Food already mentioned, there are TetraTips freeze dried food tablets. These are highly recommended as they constitute a measured supply and are also gladly taken. TetraTips are especially popular with Discus when pressed to the glass. Time and again, the fish will swim to the glass and nibble at the tablets. TetraTips also provide an effective method for administering medicaments to Discus. A few tips are ground down and mixed with the medication and a little water. This broth is then pasted onto another, whole TetraTips and allowed to dry overnight, and offered to the fish the next day. Fish which like eating TetraTips will now ingest the medication directly. TetraMedicated Food in flake form is another excellent medication system for Discus.

Not to be recommended, however, are Tubifex worms. These are already so contaminated and polluted with dirt and heavy metals that they should not be used for feeding. Large Discus do not generally take to freeze-dried mosquito larvae as these float on the surface, even when they are very small. Other mosquito larvae, such as white or black, are also available in deepfrozen form. Unfortunately, Discus seem to prefer the red variety. There is certainly an advantage, however, in familiarising Discus with black or white frozen mosquito larvae, where possible, as these two varieties are far more nutritious. Another staple feed for Discus is beef hearts. A heart free of sinews and fat is cut into small pieces and frozen.

When needed, a hard piece of beef heart can be grated on a vegetable or nut grater, and appliances are also available for this purpose. If the heart is grated in deep-frozen state small worm-like strips will result which the fish will readily take. To improve the content, the heart can be injected with vitamins or mineral preparations before being frozen. A syringe with a needle is needed for this purpose, which can be obtained from any chemist. A multi-vitamin or mineral product is placed in the syringe and injected into the meat in small doses. The meat can then be frozen. The product injected in this way is also frozen and mixed directly with the meat on thawing out. In this way, the Discus obtain enriched heart meat, an important ingredient in their diet.

Discus fish are peaceful eaters who like to take their food from the bottom. They search the tank the whole day trough for food.

Another possibility would be to remove the fat from the heart, cut it into pieces, and reduce it in a mixer, depending on the size of the fish. To this pulp a multi-vitamin mineral product, e. g. Osspulvit is similarly added. Chopped, boiled spinach, raw yolk of egg and paprika powder can be added as well.. The pulp is then put into a plastic bag, the mass distributed over a thin plate and everything is frozen. Small cubes can then be easily broken off the thin plate.

Freeze-dried mosquito larvae can also be mixed into the beef heart pulp. The larvae then absorb the moisture and descend into the tank with the hearts, where they they are then easily eaten.

Another good Discus food are Enchytraea. The hobbyist can raise the small withe worms himself. Enchytraea are taken avidly and are a good means of getting the female to spawn. However, as Enchytraea are very fatty the quantities given should be kept within bounds. The worms are invaluable for young fish as well. If, in fact, Enchytraea are fed together with highly albuminous substances, the fish will obtain important – if not essential – albumens. Vitamin powder can also be scattered on the Enchytraea cultures and the worms enriched with vitamins in this way.

Water fleas, on the other hand, are a food willingly taken only by smaller Discus. Large, adult Discus no longer bother about them.

When introducing Discus to a new food form, the Discus-keeper will have to slowly acclimate his fish to the new food by feeding them small quantities daily to start with, then slowly increasing the amount. Wether a Discus fish will take to a new food or not is very much a matter of patience on the part of the aquarist. Quality dry food has advantages which must be given due consideration. Three to four feedings a day would be ideal for large Discus. Feed little but often is the rule. Dry food in the morning or afternoon, with a portion of live or deep-frozen food in the evening. The fish should be allowed at least fifteen minutes before feeding in the morning to become really active. The Discus will still eat nothing immediately after the light is switched on. They must first regain their fine hues and the colour of the eye, in particular,

Red mosquito larvae, commercially available deep-frozen are one of the most popular sources of food for Discus. But there exist many problems with heavy metals in red mosquito larvae.

A skin secretion on the parents is the chief source of food for the fry in the first fortnight. Additional food can already be given after five days.

must be clearly visible. If it is not, it means the fish are not yet active.

Young fish in principle eat the same as an adult Discus. The young should, however, be fed several times a day, the more often the better. But only in such quantities as are quickly eaten up. Members of the family staying at home can perhaps feed them with dry food and tablets while the Discus-breeder will offer the small fish a delicacy in the early morning or at nigth, using more laborious means.

Unfortunately, small Discus cannot be left at home for days at a time without food. The damage would be too great. Someone must in fact be found who is prepared to feed them at least twice a day. This applies up to about their twelfth week. From then on, feeding once only a day will do for a period of time. Adult Discus can tolerate going hungry for a week. But it would be better if it could be avoided.

In any event, the fish should be fed more abundantly for several days before the holiday or weekend trip.

This fine Green male bred from wild-caught specimens carries only four fry which have swum freely for only a week. As this was the first successful breeding I let him continue to raise these few young.

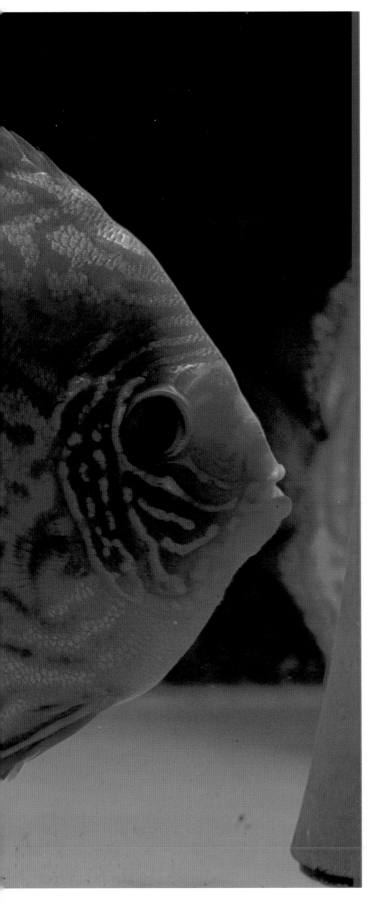

The pronounced red element in the cross stripes of this Turquoise Discus is brought out by the spotlight. It may justifiably be called a Red/Turquoise. The red colour would deepen even more if the iron content of the water is increased.

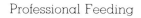

The fish portrayed in these two pictures is the same as that on the previous double-page. The differences in colouring are interesting. The Discus appears in its best light at left top, while below an other discus displays its vertical fright markings. All Discus show these dark vertical stripes to indicate submission to another Discus in territorial skirmishes.

A quick way with Discus ailments

Discus fish are not more prone to disease than any comparable fish. The complaints of Discus fish have simply been too shrouded in a veil of secrecy. As with all ornamental fishes, we must get to the root of the trouble with Discus as well. The supreme commandment in disease prevention is be sure of your water quality. We keep these fish in aquarium with several hundred litres of water while, in nature, several thousand litres flow past our Discus every minute.

Logically, the risk of the water deteriorating in a small aquarium is much greater than in nature. There is, therefore, a much greater danger of disease breaking out simply because the quality of the water is less good. This can be prevented, in turn, by regular part-water changing, large filter chambers, suitable filter substrate and nitrate filtration, so often recommended.

Factors which produce disease among aquarium fishes are ammonia and nitrite poisoning, rapid changes in the pH value, temperature drops, lack of oxygen and intoxication through foreign substances. To this may be added unsuitable transport of the fish, transfer to a new aquatic environment, overpopulation of the tank and the introduction of disease by new fish.

The food given to the fish also plays an important part as regards susceptibility to disease. The poorer a Discus eats, the more susceptible it becomes. If the food given is too uniform, often just to suit the aquarist, the fish will not be adequately provided with the right nutrients. That is why variety is important when feeding.

Fish can also be over-fed. As fishes in captivity never have the swimming space as those swimming in freedom, their overall metabolic rate must also be lower. This must be also taken into account. Fishes can, in fact, over-eat and this

produces serious disruption of the metabolsim, fatty livers, etc.

Newly acquired fish should in any event be put into quarantine. This is particularly advisable with Discus since they are, after all, expensive fish. The newcomers can be prepared with preventive treatment. Half a tablet of Cotrim Oxazole or Bactrim forte and a tablet of Flagyl or 250 mg of Metronidazol can be dissolved in 12,5 gallons (50 l) of quarantine water. The fish remain in the quarantine bath for at least five days. This tank is filtered through wadding and run on an aerator. The temperature should be 86° F (30° C). If the fish are in good condition the temperature can during these five days be raised to 90° F (32–33° C). A good supply of oxygen must then be ensured.

After this period of quarantine the new fish can be transferred to the community tank without further ado.

Many medications from human medicine are now used for Discus as well. These medications, which are very effective, are obtainable only from a pharmacy or through a vet. Many of those in human and veterinary medicine are available on prescription.

Apart from the ordinary fish diseases such as Costia and Ichthyophtirius multifiliis, for which effective medications are available trough the pet trade, there are diseases specific to the Discus. Flagellates, intestinal worms, gill worms and other parasites are a recurring nuisance with Discus. Worm infestation is common and can be detected from the white, tough excrement. Frequent chafing against ornaments in the tank is also a cause of worry to the keeper.

Each of these symptoms and the ways of treating them are referred to in the table below.

Medicaments available from pharmacies are marked with an (A).

A further, often very effective cure is to heat up the aquarium water substantially. This may prove successful, especially with white excrement and dark fish off their food. The aquarium water must be heated to 95°–97° F (35°–36° C) under careful control and with a good oxygen supply. This must be done slowly. Cool off again slowly to normal temperature after a week.

With hole-in-the-head disease, this period can be extended to 2 weeks. It will be obvious that heat treatment of this kind places a heavy burden on the fish but the success is often remarkable. However, this heat treatment may be too much for a weak, very thin fish. In the case of very sick specimens who no longer eat and who are thin and produce white excrement, the attempt of syringing Metronidazol into the mouth as described should certainly be attempted. Perseverance is necessary!

TetraMedica Hex-Ex® is an exceptionally effective treatment against tge dreaded hole-in-the head disease. It is available through any tropical fish dealer.

As the treatment of sick Discus with the food tablet mixed with medications and the administration of medications directly into the mouth with a syringe is so important, and can save the lives of many Discus, the precise procedure is again described.

Degen's Treatment for Discus

Medicines from the human range are particulary important to Discus keepers. They can be used to cure Discus rapidly of serious, fatal illnesses. Discus frequently die from an infestation with flagellates or tapeworm. We have the medicaments Flagyl and Simplotan available in this case, which are used in human medicine to control Trichomonads. The medicines are available only from a chemist. In the past, a dosage was recommended of 4 mg Flagyl per litre or 1 g of Simplotan tablet per 25 gallons (100 litres) of water. However, as apsorption through water is very poor, I have devised the following methods.

First of all, take a tablet of Simplotan or 2 tablets of Flagyl, or 500 mg of Metronidazol, rub them fine and mix them with 6 crushed food tablets. Now carefully add one drop of water to form a spreadable paste. Spread the paste over ten food tablets and leave them to dry overnight. Now administer them in the ordinary way. I have regularly given this food for preventive purposes, e. g. once a month for 2 days consecutively. If the fish are no longer taking food, they will of course be beyond recovery. That is why I developed a second, highly effective method. 500 mg of Metronidazol is dissolved in 2.5 gallons (10 l) water. For this purpose I use an empty cough mixture bottle or something similar. I then take a plastic syringe (without needle) and suck up the dissolved medicament. The fish is removed from the tank and placed on a damp towel, covered, held carefully and fed adroitly with the syringe, which is of course blunt. 2 ml is given to the fish once a day, with each feed. Give yourself time because the fish have difficulty swallowing. After feeding, wait 30 seconds before returning the fish to the tank as it will swallow once more. Some of the medicine will be spat out on its being returned. Repeat the process for 5 days. No harm will come to the fish. The medicine does no damage. This treatment will normally be sufficient and the fish will again begin to eat. But you can easily repeat the treatment with a week in between. By this means I have saved the lives of many Discus who had stopped eating. No fish has died as a result of the treatment.

Blue wild-caught Discus – Symphyso-don aequifasciatus haraldi. For a Blue Discus, this specimen already has very pronounced longitudinal stripes in the back and stomach regions.

Wild-caught Royal Blue striped all the way through. The blue of the body markings is more pronounced under weaker light. The large red proportion at the end of the fins and penants make this wild-caught fish particularly interesting.

Help with Diseases

Symptoms	Cause	Treatment
Protruding and "pop" eyes	Bacterial infection, usually also water deterioration	Immediate part-water change. 1 tablet Cotrim Oxazole (A) to 25 gall. (100 l) water, part-water change(50%) after 4 days. If no improvement by the second day, repeat half the dosage.
Clouding of the skin, milky-white clouding, white patches	Costia or Ichthyobodo necatrix	1 tablet. Cortim Oxazole (A) to 25 gall. (100 l) for 3 days at a time, then 50% water change. A further 50% water change 2 days later.
Choking, difficult breathing, nervous shooting around the tank	Gill worms	Brief bath in Masoten (poisonous) (USA Dylox) (A) under observation. 100 mg to 25 gall. (100 l) water, period 10–30 minutes if possible, or long bath in Masoten, 35 mg to 25 gall. (100 l) for 4 days. Water change after 4th day and charcoal filtration. Repeat process after 1 week.
Refusal to take food, jelly-like strings of excrement.	Threatworms Intestinal disease	Long bath in Masoten (poisonous), 35 mg to 25 gall. (100 l). Replace ¼ of the water daily and top up with a ¼ dose of Masoten. Part-water change after 4 days and charcoal filtration.
Dirty, white, long strings of excrement	Nematodes Tapeworms Fish leeches	100 mg Praziquantel (A) or 500 mg Yomesan (A) dissolved in 100 ml water, place live mosquito larvae in the solution. Feed to fishes before larvae die. Mix same dosage with 25 g flake and a little oil, feed for 5 days. Also administered with Treta Tips with coating. Dosage for 15 food tablets for 5 days. Or administer through syringe. Distribute dosage over 5 syringes of 5 ml daily each, sufficient for large discus.
Off food, very dark colour, abnormal behaviour, jelly-like excrement, hole-in-head disease – white mass exudes above eyes. Crater-like holes in the head region.	Flagellates, i. e. Hexamita, Octomitus Spironucleus	Long bath in Flagyl (A), 1 tablet (250 mg) Metronidazol in 12 gall. (50 l) water or Metronidazol as pure substance from chemists. Change 50% water after 4 days and repeat same treatment. Possibility of administration with food tablets or syringe. Or treat with TetraMedica Hex-Ex.
Skin diseases Scouring on decorative items	Bacterial skin diseases	Brief bath of 10 to 30 minutes with 150 mg Chlorampenicol (A) or 1 g Acriflavine, sold as Trypaflavin (A), per 25 gall. (100 l) for 2–3 days, then part-water change and charcoal filtration.

This Turquoise Discus had to be treated with Metronidazol, mixed in with nutrient solution.

Crater-like holes in the head region, as over the eye here, point to hole-in-the-head disease. The disease will need proper treatment.

Where is the Road leading?

Where is the road of the Discus leading? A question which is not easily answered. Will it become degraded as mass-produced goods, when the Asian dealers start flooding the market with quality, colourful fish? Will Discus then still be bred only for a fast buck? We must wait and see.

Local breeders must stay true to their line and breed up only high quality specimens. Selected breeding, maintenance of the charakteristics of the species, this is what breeders must aim for. A good shape, unflawed colouring, round, thickset specimens. These must be the hallmarks of home-bred Discus.

The road back to the pure-blooded wild-caught breeds must also be trod. Good, purebred Brown, Green and Blue wildcaught Discus must again be raised. They deserve greater attention. There may again be a market for the progeny of wildcaught specimens of good quality. Wild-caught progeny of this kind and the Turquoise and Royal Blue Discus in parallel would be a combination worth aiming for. Let us hope that the first small ads will soon re-appear in aquarist journals – ,,Wild-caught Discus offspring for sale".